First Edition Reviews

"In today's complex society, we're constantly confronted with life's challenges. Knowing the proper way to face these can turn potential problems into successes. The Utian method is a great help in the early identification of such quandaries — and in how to deal with them. The Utian book is a must read."

                        Morry J. Weiss. Chairman, American Greetings Corp.

"Dr. Utian has written a new book, as always in his clear, engaging and informative style. This is a workable tool for problem solution leading to valuable forward motion and positive interpersonal relationships. This method of problem solving reduces stress and increases productivity."

                        Lila Nachtigall MD. Professor, Obstetrics
                        and Gynecology, New York University

"This book gets down to serious business and is written for the person who has the integrity to break through every barrier. It set's the base for positive personal action. In a world full of conflicting forces, The Utian Strategy is a *must-read* book."

                        Karen Giblin. President, Red Hot Mamas North America, Inc.

"If there are two things that slow down progress and interfere with relationships, whether personal or business, it is lack of responsibility and the "need" to assign blame. Perhaps this book will provide insights to help readers see when something is their responsibility and when it is not. Readers will find help with a myriad of interpersonal relationship issues."

Susan Wysocki, WHNP-NP, FAANP. President and CEO, National Association of Nurse Practitioners in Women's Health

"Life›s problems can be vexing or bring satisfaction through good resolution. The Utian Strategy provides a logical, straightforward method to tilt the balance in favor of satisfaction. I needed to read this when I was younger!!"

Leon Speroff, MD. Professor Emeritus of Obstetrics and Gynecology, Oregon Health & Science University

"If only I had access to the Utian strategy when I began my career, it would have saved me endless effort and sleepless nights because of struggles with conflict. As is typical of Dr. Utian, he is able to take complex issues and distill them down into easy-to-read and obvious solutions, providing in a concise and exciting manner how to solve them."

Isaac Schiff MD. Chief Vincent OB/GYN at Massachusetts General Hospital and Joe Vincent Meigs Professor of Gynecology at Harvard Medical School

As a long-term colleague of Wulf Utian and admirer of his myriad accomplishments, I can only say, sign me up for any advice Wulf wants to share about life, liberty, and the pursuit of happiness. Anyone who plans to be a success needs to problem solve head-on and master the art of conflict resolution—whether in the boardroom, the backroom, or the bedroom. If Wulf is going to talk, I am going to listen!

        Cynthia A. Stuenkel, MD. Clinical Professor Medicine, University of California, San Diego

"Dr. Utian's many years in medicine have given him valuable insights into how we interact with each other. Pay attention to his advice. You will learn how to solve small problems before they become much bigger ones."

        Barbara Kantrowitz. Co-author of "The Menopause Book" (Workman Publishing 2009).

A careful analysis of how easily we allow the dilemmas created by (and belonging to) others to become our own, thus complicating our lives and our relationships. Utian's book advises on things like sensing when someone else is passing the buck, managing inter-personal relations and conflict, as well as problem solving. Not, perhaps, the most commendable response to the "am I my brother's keeper?" question, but a useful guide to navigating the messy boundaries of many 21st century relationships.

        South African Jewish Report, February 18, 2011.

The Utian Strategy provides refreshing advice on restoring professional responsibility.

        Cape Times, South Africa, January 21, 2011

IS THIS *MY* PROBLEM
OR *YOURS?*

THE UTIAN STRATEGY

3rd Edition, Newly Revised

Other Books By Wulf Utian

The Menopause Manual A Woman's Guide to the Menopause (MTP Press, Lancaster, 1978)

Menopause in Modern Perspective (AppletonCenturyCrofts, 1980)

Your Middle Years: A Doctor's Guide for Today's Woman (AppletonCenturyCrofts, 1980)

The Premenstrual Syndrome. Pieter van Keep, Wulf H. Utian (MTP Press, Lancs. 1981)

The Controversial Climacteric. Pieter van Keep, Wulf H. Utian, Alex Vermuelen (MTP Press, Lancs. 1982)

Multidisciplinary Perspectives on Menopause. Marcha Flint, Fredi Kronenberg, Wulf Utian (Annals of the New York Academy of Sciences, Volume 592, June 13, 1990)

Managing Your Menopause. Wulf H. Utian and Ruth S. Jacobowitz (Prentice Hall Press, New York, 1990)

The Menopause and Hormonal Replacement Therapy - Facts and Controversies. Regine Sitruk-Ware and Wulf H. Utian (Marcel Dekker, Inc., New York, 1991)

FINDING THE UNEXPECTED – Searching Utian Family Roots in Lithuania. (The Utian Press, Cleveland, 2014)

CHANGE YOUR MENOPAUSE! Why one size does not fit all. (The Utian Press, Cleveland, 2016)

IS THIS *MY* PROBLEM OR *YOURS*?

THE UTIAN STRATEGY

How to recognize and resolve potential problems or interpersonal conflict at home, at work, at large, by ascribing ownership and using interpersonal communication – and even to convert problems into personal advantage

Wulf H. Utian
MD, PhD. DSc (Med), FRCOG, FACOG, FICS

UTIAN PRESS
Beachwood, Ohio
www.UtianLLC.com

Copyright © 2010, 2011, 2020 by Wulf H. Utian
All rights reserved. Except as permitted under the
U.S. Copyright Act of 1976, no part of this publication
may be reproduced, distributed or transmitted in any form
or by any means, or stored in a database or retrieval system,
without the prior permission of the author.

First Edition October 2010
ISBN 978-0-9828457-0-7 (print edition)

Second Edition October 2011
ISBN 978-0-9828457-1-4 (eBook)

Third Edition November 2020
ISBN 978-0-9909160-0-0 (print edition)
ISBN 978-0-9909160-1-7 (eBook)

Library of Congress Control Number: 2010911080

Library of Congress Subject Headings:
Conflict management.
Interpersonal communication.
Interpersonal conflict.
Problem solving.
Problem solving – case studies.

To Moira, my wife of 54 years, for an exciting life, and for constantly cajoling me that life is not a dress rehearsal

Author's Biographical Sketch

Wulf H. Utian, MD, PhD, DSc.
Professor Emeritus of Reproductive Biology and OB/GYN, Case Western Reserve University School of Medicine

Consultant in Women's Health, The Cleveland Clinic

Scientific Director Emeritus, Rapid Medical Research, Inc.

Dr. Utian received his medical degree from the University of Witwatersrand, Johannesburg, South Africa (1962), and his PhD (1970) and DSc (2007) from the University of Cape Town, South Africa He is Board Certified in Obstetrics and Gynecology and Reproductive Endocrinology, and is a Fellow of the Royal College of Obstetricians and Gynaecologists, the American College of Obstetricians and Gynecologists, and the International College of Surgeons. He was Director of the Department of Obstetrics and Gynecology, University Hospitals of Cleveland (1989-1999), and Chairman of the Department of Reproductive Biology, Case Western Reserve University (1989-1999).

Dr. Utian is a specialist in the fields of gynecological endocrinology and infertility. He has been an innovator in several aspects of advanced reproductive technology, including leading the team to achieve the world's first surrogate in vitro fertilization pregnancy in the world. He has studied the metabolic and psychosocial aspects of estrogen and menopause for over 50 years. In 1967, he established the Groote Schuur Menopause Research Clinic in Cape Town, South Africa, the world's first such clinic. He is the Co-Founder of the International Menopause Society (IMS), and Founder of the North American Menopause Society (NAMS).

A strong advocate for women's health, Dr. Utian has achieved international recognition for his work and is interviewed regularly by the international media. He was honored by *Good Housekeeping* magazine in 1997 as "one of America's best physicians in women's health," by *Ladies Home Journal* in 1999 as one of the "top ten researchers in women's health," was the first recipient of the NAMS Lifetime Achievement Award in 1999, was honored by the Royal College of Obstetricians and Gynaecologists in 2000 for his achievements in the area of menopause, and in 2005 was awarded the Food and Drug Administration's Commissioner's Special Citation "for the collective outstanding performance of the 'Menopause and Hormones Information Campaign' that resulted in the launch of a national public awareness outreach campaign," in Canada in 2013 with the first SIGMA/Canadian Menopause Society "Menopause Trail Blazer Award", in 2017 with the Establishment of an Annual Wulf Utian IMS/CAMS Award for Achievement in Furthering Women's Health presented to "any member who does great work in their own country to further education on menopause," and received the Lifetime Achievement Award of the IMS in 2020.

His most recent book takes him back to his medical roots, *CHANGE YOUR MENOPAUSE! Why one size does not fit all.*

Complete resume and communication information: www.UtianLLC.com

Preface To 3rd Edition

There is life pre-Covid-19 and life after Covid-19. The first editions of this "how-to" book were clearly written before we were all so adversely impacted by this horrific pandemic.

We as individuals are not responsible for the existence of the virus. We are responsible for our personal actions in relation to the pandemic. Our governments are obviously responsible for accepting ownership of the problem and driving mitigation policies. But have they taken ownership of the problem, or left us swinging in the wind, in effect making their problem our problem?

If this book had relevance before, it's philosophy has even greater relevance now.

My best wishes
Wulf Utian
Cape Town, South Africa, and Cleveland, Ohio
November 2020

Contents

	Author's Biographical Sketch xi	
	Preface To 3rd Edition xiii	
	Introduction 1	
Chapter 1	The Utian Strategy – Defining Problems and Problem Ownership 3	
Chapter 2	Personal and Family Life 9	
Chapter 3	Race and Politics 31	
Chapter 4	The Workplace 49	
Chapter 5	Health and Healthcare 63	
Chapter 6	The Inverse Utian Strategy – Your Pathway to Success 75	
Chapter 7	Tell Them It Is Their Problem – Fix It! 81	
Chapter 8	Summing Up the Utian Strategy 85	
	Notes 91	
	How to Order 93	
	Share An Experience of Your Own 94	

Introduction

"We have a problem!!"

Ever heard those words – from a family member, a friend, or an employee?

And how often have you taken the bait – finding yourself inevitably trapped, cornered, snookered – indeed, left with owning and dealing with a problem that was never yours to begin with?

That is what this book is about – how instantly to recognize a problem, to smell a rat, to sense someone is passing the buck, and for you to rapidly determine whether you truly own the problem. The Utian Strategy is the process of considering, defining, and determining a response to the simple question: Is this my problem or is this your problem?

Through dozens of personal experiences – at home, at work, in health care, in department and business administration – I developed a philosophy of problem resolution, through identification of problem ownership. So what is the trick to avoiding traps, recognizing the emergence of a problem, resolving the problem through true disposition of ownership, and even in some instances of turning the problem to personal advantage?

Simply put, the Utian Strategy alerts you to instantly make yourself aware of an impending problem, dilemma, or arising conflict, then to immediately ask yourself the question "Is this my problem or is this your problem?" Then, either take ownership of the problem or deny ownership.

How does this work? Read on as I share the Utian Strategy with you through a series of examples and vignettes, many based on my own life experiences……

Chapter 1

The Utian Strategy – Defining Problems and Problem Ownership

I learned my lessons in the school of hard knocks – the real world. The most significant lesson learned was how to recognize and effectively manage problems. In a few brief readable pages I share this technique with you through this semi-biographical book that could change your life for the better. This is a formula for taking control. Life's dilemmas or interpersonal problems have logic. Applying that logic to life's day-to-day problems puts you in the driver's seat.

Let's define the word 'problem.' It is a noun meaning a 'doubtful or difficult matter requiring a solution,' or 'something hard to understand or accomplish.' (The Pocket Oxford Dictionary). So the Utian Strategy is a method to help you determine who owns the problem and therefore has the responsibility of finding and accomplishing the solution. Is the problem yours, or is the problem someone else's?

My eureka moment came somewhere in southern France in 1964. Fresh out of a one-year medical/surgical internship following graduation from medical school in 1962 in Johannesburg, South Africa, I recognized that I knew a lot about medicine and pathetically little about life and the bigger world. Bitten by a travel bug from the age of six or seven and driven to explore new cultures, I packed a rucksack and set off on a one-year solo "backpackers" trip through Africa, every country in Western Europe, Poland, Russia and then Greece and Israel.

The year 1964 was not yet the time of the global hitchhiker. The swarms of young travelers to Europe would come later. Being a pioneer had its moments – sometimes the feast of meeting fascinating people; sometimes the famine of essentially being alone days on end and speaking English to no one.

My only languages were English and Afrikaans, the Dutch dialect of South Africa, and this meant problems in Europe. In France particularly, no one seemed to want to speak English. It was during one of the famine periods that I found myself alone in a small village in southern France, wanting to head towards Nice, and finding no signposts at a fork in the road. Clearly I could not take Yogi Berra's advice, 'when you come to a fork in the road, take it!' Fortunately there were a few villagers about doing whatever they were about, and I approached a young man, assuming that he must speak some English, but aware, from several previous unsuccessful attempts, of the French's apparent aversion to English. Feeling desperate, my mind was racing with strategies – when an idea struck me. I had a problem – I needed directions. The French had a problem – they did not seem to want to speak English or, in fairness, were not able. How could I resolve the dilemma? This problem with the French was negatively impacting on me. My resolution was a devious compromise. I approached the young Frenchman and addressed him in Afrikaans – "Goie more meneer, can meneer vir my asseblief die pad na Nice wys?" (Good morning sir, could you please direct me to the road to Nice?). Of course I knew there was no way on earth a young small-town Frenchman could understand Afrikaans. He looked at me blankly. Then I continued in a faked deeply accented English – "perhaps you speak English, yes?" He nodded – "a little." "Excellent", I responded, got the correct directions and continued on my way.

It was early in the year and I had been fleeing the cold of northern Europe, a cold I had never experienced before in my life – definitely nothing like that exists in South Africa. Days later, warmer, happier and wondering along the coast of the French Riviera, I sat on a bench overlooking a crop of rocks butting into the sea. The gentle, variable and relentless roll of the incoming waves set me to thinking about my travel experiences, and I replayed in my mind my conversation those days before. The logic of the waves suggested to me that there was a logic in the way I had resolved my problem of finding my way.

Here was a real interpersonal conflict. The Frenchman had a problem – most likely not wanting to expose his poor English to an "Englishman". I had a problem – I needed directions. However, he was essentially compounding my problems by making his problem my problem. There was absolutely and definitely a nice logic in all of this – a lesson to be learned, a technique for interpersonal problem-solving that could be developed.

Of course, it was really very simple! A set of elemental but logical issues struck home.

1. Problems or potential problems need to be recognized, dissected and analyzed into their basic issues.
2. Problems have ownership.
3. The person with the problem will often try to transfer ownership, converting their problem into our problem.
4. Recognition that a problem exists is essential, and awareness of potential problem transfer mandatory.

5. Resolution of the situation necessitates recognition of the above, especially identifying who owns the problem.
6. Once ownership is assigned, the responsibility is on the owner to seek the solution.

In simple terms, I had come up with a mechanism of interpersonal problem resolution that I have stuck to throughout my life. While I certainly cannot claim 100% success in problem conflict resolution, sticking to my guns more often than not helped all parties concerned get over the issue and on with their lives.

Was this intuitive or really an eureka moment? Not important. What I had recognized was that life situations have an exquisite logic. This is the case despite the "human element" which invariably is to allow the heart, that is emotion, override the brain, the application of common sense. The purpose then of this somewhat autobiographical book is to share with you the power of logic in problem resolution, be it in family matters, on the job, relating to healthcare, education, or love life and personal relations.

The Utian Strategy is simple. Whatever the situation, always run the following questions through your mind. The answers will provide a logical direct path to resolution.

1. Recognize that a problem is developing or exists. (Is there a problem?)
2. Define the problem – what exactly are the issues, the facts and nothing but the facts?
3. Ask yourself the question – is this my problem or is this your problem (the other party)? (Who owns the problem?)

4. Consider the situation – is the opposite party trying to make their problem your problem?
5. Consider the reverse – am I attempting to pass the buck by making my problem belong to someone else?
6. The owner takes possession. Go away and solve the problem.

Help, advice, comfort and assistance can be offered, but the owner of the problem must develop the solution and take the appropriate step to resolve it. Not to do so can have unfortunate consequences.

There are clearly countless problems with multiple potential combinations and permutations. Life is really a series of problems that arise continuously. While the possibilities might be endless, the technique to recognizing the nature and existence of a problem and assigning ownership and responsibility for dealing with it is logical, similar and usually quite easy. It most certainly requires clear thinking and an ability to be assertive, to take a position!

In the following chapters, I will share examples with you, many of them personal experiences, as we consider applying these questions to some of life's different components and circumstances. My own experiences have been diverse – not always successful – but certainly serve as good illustrations of comprehending and applying my Utian Strategy. Recognize that the examples, although seeming to relate to one particular situation, say a family problem, invariably offer tactics that could be applied to another situation, for example a problem at work.

Chapter 2

Personal and Family Life

Parents and Children

An extreme example of problem transference occurred in my own family. My late father, who was a kind, generous, chronically ill and very complicated man, was born in a town called Possville, near another town called Utian, on the border of Russia and Lithuania. Pogroms, poverty and parents wanting better for at least some of their children, led to two young boys, my father and his older brother, being sent via London to South Africa, where a family member had preceded them. Parentless, penniless and speaking only Russian and Yiddish, the two young boys developed their life's careers, my father first in Pretoria and then in Johannesburg. He was apprenticed to a manufacturing jeweler, and ultimately opened his own factory/studio becoming nationally famous for the quality of his artistry and workmanship and his intimate knowledge of diamonds. Above all, he was known as a man of complete honesty – every negotiation or agreement settled on a handshake – "mazel and brocha" – "good luck and blessings." So great were his skills, in 1948 he was commissioned by the DeBeers organization to create a large broach that was to be presented as a gift to Queen Elizabeth I, during their royal visit to South Africa, a spray of flowers, with each flower being a magnificent diamond. I am certain the piece resides to this day in Queen Elizabeth II's crown jewels.

At that time his bad luck was to develop a duodenal peptic ulcer in those years of surgical therapy well before the "taken for granted" era of modern medications. One complicated surgery after another led to a need to return for yet another surgical procedure and this necessitated travelling from Johannesburg to Durban, a distance of 400 miles. On the road, he fell asleep at the wheel of his car, drove off a cliff, fractured his skull, stove in his chest, ruptured his diaphragm and was admitted to a hospital in a small town about 100 miles from home. My mother left immediately to join him. I was pulled out of school and followed later in the day with my uncle and aunt. They were allowed into the small cottage hospital and I was told to go and play outside. In the garden, I was aware of only one thing – the wailing of my father in total agony. He screamed and screamed. I was agitated. I walked up and down near the window from which the pain was emanating. My father's problem was instantly my problem, and I truly believe it was at that moment I decided to become a physician. I have had a great career, do not regret one moment of it, and in this instance, the transference of ownership of a problem had a positive outcome.

My younger brother was not so lucky. There is a five-year age gap between myself and my brother, and my sister is two years younger than him. From the moment he could handle toy wooden blocks he built bridges. He was also artistic, with enormous talent for drawing and painting. Talent he was certainly not short of. But he was a victim of my father's circumstances.

My brother eventually decided he wanted to be an engineer. His mathematical and artistical skills would seem to have made him a natural for that career path. My father thought otherwise. "There are no Jewish engineers" he would shout whenever the subject came up for discussion.

"Jews are doctors and lawyers and accountants – no construction company in Johannesburg will hire a Jewish engineer. You will qualify and be jobless and how could you start anything alone?!" and on, and on, and on went this relentless harangue. Eventually my brother bowed to the inevitable, went to the Witwatersrand University in Johannesburg, graduated with an accountant degree and entered an accounting practice. He hated it. Dull numbers and no dreams. No designing, no building, no contractors, no barriers to break. Just numbers.

The inevitable became the actual. He gave up the accounting practice, went into a series of businesses, some successful, some quite the opposite, searching for something but never quite finding it.

My father had a problem – whatever it was. Clearly he had fixed ideas about his son's career plans and possibilities. He forced his problem on to my brother, who became the victim.

It is so simple to be a Monday morning quarterback, to look back through the retrospectoscope, and to think how easy it should have been to resolve this situation. It happened, and it is history, but a lesson for others comes out of it:

Don't let someone else make their problem your problem.

Hindsight should be 20/20. Having observed this, developed an understanding of the "my problem/your problem?" strategy in my early 20's, I should have been the world's most successful parent. Actually we have two children who are now adults, well established in remarkable careers, and with whom I have an ideal relationship – warm, open, intellectual, problem-sharing, great conversation and love, in short, everything any parent could possibly desire as a family outcome. Getting there was another story.

We first arrived in the United States from South Africa in July 1976. In fact we celebrated the Bicentennial at a concert in London at the London Palladium with Bing Crosby and Rosemary Clooney. People always say moving from one city to another, or one country to another, is easy on the children because they adapt quickly. This is not necessarily true. Cape Town, South Africa, to Cleveland, Ohio was a shock to our systems and equally to the children's. As a family we were very close. Indeed, the first couple of years we were broke, surviving from paycheck to paycheck. Living in a rented side by side, our living room furniture comprised of two armchairs and an old TV set on a small stand. The evenings were spent together as a family – the chairs shared in two by two with switching at various intervals. Circumstances were difficult – we had left our parents, siblings and large circle of friends, the complete environment for our children, to become strangers in a foreign land knowing just a handful of people. School was different and the children inevitably had problems in adapting. While we spoke South African English (that is, English with a South African accent) and the Americans spoke American English (that is, American with an American accent), the same words often had different meanings.

That reminds me of an embarrassing experience – nothing to do with my strategy – but which itself could have been a "problem." When I arrived to start my Sabbatical at University Hospitals of Cleveland, the chairman, Brian Little, introduced me to the secretarial staff who at that time sat together at desks banked together in a pool area. He provided me with an office, at least one I shared with another faculty member, who used a fair amount of space to store his bicycle, extra pairs of Texas boots and other sundry items. At least I had a good size desk! I was planning to use my Sabbatical to write my first book (and in fact completed two, one for physicians and one for consumers) and wanted to get right to it. Brian introduced me to one of the secretaries in the pool, an older woman who was the senior administrative secretary and advised me that she would help me get an office established.

I dumped my notes on the desk, a half dozen legal pads, several pencils, and got right down to work. But something was missing, so I walked down the hallway to the secretarial pool and asked of the women sitting there "does anyone here have a rubber?" Rather than an offer of help, there was a stunned and shocked silence. All the women looked at me in a very strange manner. My new secretary took me aside and said, "what exactly is it that you want?" "A rubber", I answered, "something to rub out errors on the page as I write my book with a pencil." "Oh" she said understandingly. "Look, in America we call that an eraser. Here, a rubber is a condom!" I never did get follow-up from the other secretaries as to what they thought of this South African male and his odd request on his first day on the job!

Other examples abound. If I said I would do something "just now", I meant, in a while, and wondered why someone would continue to stand around waiting. "Quite nice" in English meant just okay; in America it meant pretty good. A lift was an elevator, a boot was a car trunk, the pavement a sidewalk, "how are you?" a greeting and not really a question.

Of course Americans are the most open and friendly people in the world. Not long after we settled in Cleveland my mother came to visit. Returning from the stores with my wife she remarked to me, "you have been here such a short time and already Moira seems to know everybody!" "How so?" I responded. "Well, everyone we passed asked Moira – how are you!" What we all realized early on was that even unintended misuse or misunderstanding of language could generate a problem. Watch your words!

As a family we became very aware of local problems, national politics and international affairs. We would debate and discuss all the events of the day down to the finest detail. The kids were exposed to everything. Lara was all of six years old when, during a visit to Cleveland by Moira's parents, Lara, observing a TV news item said "Grandpa, that woman is a prostitute." Silence followed, and Lara questioned "Grandpa, do you know what a prostitute is?" When he nodded his head, she observed "I think it is pretty sad that a woman has to earn a living that way."

Over the next few years, and a couple of house moves, Brett became more and more conservative in his politics; Lara became the ultimate liberal. Brett was to the right of Attila the Hun and Lara was to the left of Mother Theresa. She initiated a chapter of Amnesty International at her high school, and the house was constantly being visited by Green Peace, Save the Whale, Pro-Choice, Amnesty International, and every fringe element conceivable. Brett would complain, "have you seen those commies she keeps bringing home!"

It was against this background that we were faced with the problems and crises that needed resolving.

Lessons Learned
1. It is very simple to advise someone else what to do; following your own advice is not that easy.
2. The Utian Strategy will not work if you get emotionally involved.

My excuse for not following my own guidelines in raising our children after our move was that I had a sense of guilt for having taken them from a friendly to a strange and sometimes hostile environment. What that meant was that my wife and I became overly protective, taking ownership of problems the children should have been taught to deal with. Of course most of these issues in the greater scheme of things were trivial (at least in retrospect), but it is the principle that counts. Do you recognize any similarity with the way you are raising your own children?

Here is a good example, because it happened more recently with my daughter. Yes, family problems don't disappear as we all age – kids remain our kids forever, it seems to me.

My daughter is back in South Africa, at that time living in Johannesburg – strange irony, no?! Anyway, my wife and I were in Cape Town, about 1,000 miles away. We were due to fly to Johannesburg in a couple of days to spend time with Lara. I am driving on the freeway and my cell phone goes –

"Dad, I just had an accident!"

"Are you okay?"

"Yes, I am fine, shaken up, but the car is a mess – you will have to drive us in Johannesburg, when you are here."

"But Lara, I had no plans to rent a car in Johannesburg."

"Well you will have to!"

"No, Lara, I do not want to drive, but you rent a car."

"I don't have the money."

"Okay, I'll pay for it."

Analysis

Consider the above discussion. I have been snookered by my daughter, who over the years has learned to handle the Utian Strategy (don't allow the other party make their problem our problem) and the Inverse Utian Strategy (use every trick in the book to make our problem their problem).

Reread the above interchange and you will notice how Lara calls with her problem –" I have had an accident" - then says I must drive – that is, tries to make her problem mine. I returned the ball to her court – "no you rent a car." The ball comes right back! "I don't have the money." So I agree to pay. Bingo! I have essentially accepted her problem, aware of what has just gone on, but not wanting to upset her anymore, beyond the stress I hear in her voice about having been involved in an accident. My heart overruled my mind.

But what were my real mistakes?
1. I wanted so much for them to be happy and to achieve; I made my problem their problem.

2. They had experiences and conflicts that were personally difficult for them to deal with – and then I allowed them to make their problems my problem.

The good news is that despite missteps and errors, things did work out well. But we did learn gradually to explain to Brett and Lara that problems were issues that could be analyzed, accepted and resolved. Over time, more and more, we would have a discussion, defining the problems, ascribing ownership, and strategizing methods of resolution.

Believe me, not every session worked out. But every session that failed, that resulted in words we wished were not spoken, anger, tears or walking away, yes, every one of those problems was where emotion was allowed to trump logic and common sense. The heart overruled the mind.

Tactics Offered

1. In dealing with family issues, try and keep cool.
2. If emotion begins to creep in – "take 5". Call a time out, and say, "let's try and relax, think about things, and then start again."
3. Bite your tongue. As much as you have the urge to respond with a clever response, don't say it. Errors of commission are far worse than errors of omission. Things said cannot be taken back.
4. Keep your eye on the prize! Together, with a warm, concerned approach, work out, "Is this your problem, or is this my problem?"
5. Then, ownership of the problem accepted, work together to plan a strategy for problem resolution. Getting your child to accept their problems in a nurturing and supportive environment is always going to be the best formula for success.
6. Be certain that parents are on the same page – kids are aware of the slightest sign of disagreement, or play parents against each other, and a child's minor problems can become a major family squabble. The problems, more often than not, are trivial, but important in the children's mind,

and when resolved, family bonds will be strengthened in the process.

7. Finally, try and recognize those situations where all the children want is a sounding board, a forum to vent frustration, a desire to be understood, recognized and appreciated. Under those circumstances don't speak about problems, indeed don't speak at all. Just listen and nod.

Husband and Wife

We have now been married for over 54 years, still love each other, and have had thousands of arguments. Does the Utian Strategy work in the husband and wife context? Well, only with extreme difficulty. Emotion is the enemy. Angry words are the weapons and cause of pain and insult. Once thrown out, like bullets, they cannot be retrieved.

Suggestion:

1. Try harder to listen and not respond.

2. Constantly search for the answer to the question
    » What is the crux of the problem?
    » Is this my problem, my spouse's problem, or a family problem?

3. Always try jointly to develop a solution – compromise is invariably the only way out.

Examples of Frequent Situations

1. *Working Husband and Homemaker Wife*

Here is a very frequent problem. The husband works away from home, whether white-collar professional or blue-collar laborer, and the wife has to cope with the day-to-day housekeeping issues and children's problems, even if she herself has another day job. Her husband returns home exhausted and harassed, and assumes that his wife has been home all day, has an easier life, and should respond to his needs immediately. Invariably, the wife accepts the unbalanced situation.

The Issue

1. Lack of respect for spouse.
2. Husband brings his problems home and makes them a wife/family problem.
3. Wife assumes ownership of the problem.
4. The situation gets worse and leads to disagreement, argument and sometimes to divorce.

The Solution

This is a situation that really needs airing. The problem has to be spelled out and ownership identified. Unfortunately, it can place a vulnerable wife, not the wage earner, in a sensitive position. She may need a referee.

Lesson

Try one on one calm discussion. "Listen Joe, I know you work hard, and have hundreds of frustrations on the job, but you are bringing your problems home and making them mine and the kids. You are also not recognizing that I have problems at home and with the kids that I don't bother you with because I know how you feel when you get home, and I don't want to burden you with my problems. I respect you, and you need to respect me. We both have problems, and we both need to solve our own problems. If you want to discuss your problems, I am more than willing to listen. But we need to be calm, not get angry and work as a team."

Some husbands just won't get it. At that time, it may be necessary to bring in a referee – a marital counselor early in the crisis can rescue a failing relationship.

2. One Spouse Controls the Purse Strings

He who has the money has the power. Nothing can be more disruptive to marital equity than squabbles over money. Control could arise in multiple ways not necessarily only when one partner is the sole wage earner. For example, one partner may have wealth from parents or inheritance; both partners may work but merge their incomes into one account with one partner dominating control of the account.

Problem

This is a really tough one. Whose problem is it?

- » The dominant monetary partner forces the lesser partner in essence to beg for money
- » The lesser partner has a problem, a dominant spouse and the need for money

To me, this appears to be a situation where there is a problem belonging to the couple and ownership cannot be allocated. But the dominant partner is almost certainly not going to offer to open any discussion.

Initially, the lesser partner needs to take the bull by the horns and call for a discussion. If fear of confrontation is a factor, a third-party counselor might be the remedy.

The Solution

The tactical approach to resolution, nonetheless, should remain the same.

1. Call for discussion – obviously the lesser partner raising the issue. "We have a problem!"
2. Air the problem – "control of money is the problem."
3. Consider tactics for problem solving - "we need to work out some sort of system so that I don't feel like I am nagging you or begging you for money."
4. Explain that marriage is a partnership and not a master/servant relationship
5. Having identified and aired the problem, offer a concrete suggestion – "I feel that we need to open a separate bank account in my name and agree on an amount that will be deposited monthly. I will use this for housekeeping and personal needs. That way, we can get all the unpleasant day-to-day requests for money out of our conversation. Truly, this will enhance our partnership."

3. The Squanderer or Gambler

The following is a family problem but serves as a terrific example of how work and family are so often intertwined.

My father had a manufacturing jewelry factory in Johannesburg. I used to spend Saturday mornings as a young boy watching the jewelers at work and learning to fabricate simple items with gold and silver. Saturday was also the weekly payday. One of my early memories was the arrangement my father had worked out with one of his most gifted workmen. Peter was a compulsive gambler. He would take his pay envelope and head directly for the racetrack and the Saturday afternoon horse races. Nine times out of ten he would go home broke, and Monday morning his wife would be in the office begging for an advance on the next week's salary.

Here was a situation where the problem clearly belonged to Peter – he was the compulsive gambler. But he had successfully transferred ownership to his wife – a problem of no money to meet household expenses. My father, too, was drawn into the problem.

In this instance, in retrospect, I now appreciate my father's approach. He assumed the role of referee of the problem. His solution he essentially imposed is that Peter's wife would come to the factory at noon on Saturdays and take direct possession of the pay envelope. Whether some of the money was to be given to Joe to gamble, was an issue between them. But his wife no longer had a problem of keeping the household together.

Lesson
1. An observer, especially one in an influential position, can play an important role as referee.
2. The reluctant owner of the problem might need to have a resolution forced on him.

4. Divorce with children

Disagreements over arrangements with children following divorce can be the most complex to resolve, ascribing ownership being sometimes almost impossible. Take the following case illustration. Phillip and Patricia divorced after one year of marriage. The courts granted custody of their three-month-old daughter to Patricia – but as the child grew up, visiting rights were given to Phillip. When the child was five years old, a further court order allowed Phillip to have the child stay over every other weekend.

Over time, the relationship between Phillip and Patricia became progressively more hostile, starting from a pretty poor base anyway. The only time they had contact was when Phillip collected the child every other Friday, and brought her back on the Sunday evening.

Phillip became concerned that his daughter seemed to have a learning disorder and was not doing well at school. Patricia took this as a personal insult and refused to discuss the issue. Phillip offered to pay for counseling and extra lessons. Patricia told him to back off. The more Phillip tried, the more Patricia resisted. Eventually, Phillip threatened to take the issue to court.

Analysis

Where does one start to define this problem – what is the problem; and whose problem is it. The apparent problem is that a child, caught in a conflict between parents, is failing to progress in school. But is this really the problem? Are there not more fundamental problems? We could list some:

1. A problem of conflicting parents and no communication.
2. A child who really has a learning disorder.

3. A battle for control over the child's affection and future.
4. A father fearful of losing parental rights.
5. An ex-wife wanting to punish an ex-husband through control of the child.

There are probably more.

Objective

The objective, presumably of both parents is to raise the child into a happy and independent adult.

A problem 'en route' is to determine whether the child has a specific learning disorder, or is failing to progress because of personality issues subsequent to family conflict.

Tactics

The ideal would be for the ex-husband and wife to behave responsibly, accept the nature of the problem, and work out an acceptable approach to resolve it. But that is fantasy in this instance – the real-world situation is that there is just too much anger for this to happen.

Another approach would be for the angry participants to accept a mediator, but before being involved in the legal system. Probably, again, this is just wishful thinking.

So the Question – Who's Problem?

This situation is so complex it would be impossible to simply say "this is your problem – don't make this my problem."

Bottom line – this is a problem that belongs to all three participants, mother, father and child.

Outcome

When a problem is communal, and the participants not willing to communicate, resolution is invariably just not achieved. The debate goes on, the fighting progressively more acrimonious, and eventually one or the other participant walks away.

This is the most likely outcome of the above example – the father eventually shrugs and walks away, the mother could do the same, but having custody is less likely to do so, or, and this will be the eventual outcome, the child grows up and enters the real world, less well prepared perhaps then she could have been. Regrettably not all problems can be resolved.

Extended Family

Family squabbles can present a real challenge. They are invariably not only difficult to analyze, but are fraught with combative emotions. Here is an interesting example that raises multiple issues and illustrates how complex even trivial issues can become.

This is a real family situation. For most Jews, even those who are not deeply observant, the Friday evening Sabbath meal is the most important family gathering of the week. The following situation developed when a sister, her husband and family, moved 1,000 miles to live near her younger sister and family. I will call the two sisters Mary and Joan, Mary being the newcomer to town. Mary was welcomed, and her family was regularly invited to Friday night dinner. She was also welcomed into the family of Joan's sister-in-law, Sally. About a year after arriving in town, Mary's daughter was to be married. As so often happens, planning the wedding became a logistical nightmare. The venue chosen for the reception was small, allowing only a limited number of guests, mostly to keep the costs down within the limits they could afford. Mary consulted with her sister Joan, asking whether she thought that Sally would be offended if their son, who was not really friendly with Mary's daughter, was not invited. Joan, in good faith, considered the question and answered that it would be very unlikely for Sally to take offense.

Of course the invitations went out and Sally and her husband sent an RSVP that they would not attend. Mary called Joan who reassured her that they were probably going to be out of town. Nonetheless, Joan called Sally and got an earful. "We are hurt, offended, insulted, after all we did to welcome that family when they came to town". And so on and so on. Such are the small issues out of which large family feuds emanate. Despite Joan's assurances that there was no malice meant, that the venue could only hold 50 people, that Mary loved Sally and her family and was appreciative of everything, none of the arguments could dampen Sally's self-righteous anger.

The issue then became more complicated a couple of weeks later when Joan invited Mary and Sally's families to their home for the Friday Sabbath dinner. Sally responds, "I am not coming to your house if they are there – thank you but count us out!" Distraught, Joan calls Mary to see if there is some way that can resolve this problem. Mary becomes hysterical, saying "I moved with my whole family to this city to be with you all, now I am causing a split in the family, and I can't deal with this and I am going to move us all back to where we came from!"

Analysis

Let's "take five", and consider this situation. The problem itself, to some, may appear trivial, but if you were a counselor, how would you advise this family?

Always start by dissecting the problem to its core elements. What is the problem? Clearly, a family wedding was held in a venue too small to accommodate all the family members. This could have been truly a physical space issue. It could just as well, for many people, have been relating to cost, and what the party givers could afford.

Other elements have intruded into the core problem:

1. Mary, the mother of the bride, had asked Joan, her sister, whether Sally, Joan's sister in law, would be offended.
2. Joan had responded, most likely not.
3. Sally was deeply offended, and she and her husband did not attend the wedding.
4. Subsequently, Sally declined Joan's invitation to Friday Sabbath dinner, if Mary and family were to be present.

So, who has ownership of this problem, or are there multiple problems with different ownership? The answer:

1. The core problem is Mary's – for whatever reason, she chose a venue too small to accommodate all family members.
2. Joan allowed Mary to make her problem Joan's problem – "do you think Sally will be offended." "Probably not."
3. Sally compounds the problem by not accepting the invitation, and then following up by declining Joan's invitation for the family Sabbath dinner.

- Now they are all scrapping with each other!

Ownership

Ownership of the problem is primarily Mary's in the way she chose the venue and sent the invitations. The victim – Joan for allowing Mary's problem to become hers.

The antagonist – Sally, who cannot or will not accept an explanation or an apology.

So how do we get to resolution?

A Monday morning quarterback would have seen this coming a mile away.

The first error was Mary's – asking Joan what Sally would think. Why not just be honest and direct and call Sally herself, explain the situation, and ask her if she would be upset?

The second error was Joan's – when asked the question by Mary, her response should have been, "I don't know. Why don't you ask Sally?" By assuming what Sally might think about the non-invitation of her son to the wedding, Joan had automatically become a player in the drama. She had allowed transference of Mary's problem to herself.

The third error was of course Sally's. Declining the invitation to Friday's Sabbath dinner, she was punishing the entire greater family for an issue that was largely between her and Mary. Was this a separate problem? Not really, because it all related to the core problem. Her correct approach would have been to accept the dinner invitation, deal with Mary in a more one to one way, either by saying "you know you really hurt and offended us" or by simply choosing to ignore her. Not an ideal situation, but emotion in family matters invariably trumps common sense.

But all of the above, beyond ascribing problem ownership, is rhetoric, "what could have been if only . . . ." Instead, we have an active problem.

Who do you think should now take ownership and get this tangle sorted out? Mary, Joan or Sally?

The problem is Mary's, Joan has allowed ownership to be transferred to herself, and Sally has compounded the conflict.

As I will constantly remind you throughout this book, firstly, try and recognize a potential interpersonal conflict or problem the moment it surfaces. Do not let the opposite party transfer ownership of the problem to you; otherwise, it will indeed become your problem. Bearing this in mind, in my opinion, at this stage, Joan has assumed ownership and must now try and resolve the problem. But how?

Once she has dissected the problem to its core essentials, which by now do not need repeating, and assuredly she has recognized, she must work out a game plan. Problem resolution usually means dealing with it and laying it to rest, not transferring it back to the other party. Sometimes, of course, if the opposite party will not "negotiate", there may be no alternate.

Joan could take the following steps:

1. Call Mary, tell her to recognize she started this, is the rightful owner of the problem, and should call Sally and apologize, eat humble pie, and let life move on.

2. Call Sally, outline her call to Mary, indicate the apology is coming, the gracious thing to do is to accept, and to recognize that failure to do so is compounding the problem into a family splitting feud.

3. Joan should also advise both Mary and Sally that both their families will continue to be invited to future Sabbath dinners, she will not tell either of them whether the opposite party has accepted or rejected the invitation, and that life will go on. If either declines the invitation, that is a new problem, and belongs to the decliner.

The outcome? I never really heard anymore beyond that, but the assumption is that they are once again a greater family, and being so, more problems will recur in the future. Hopefully, a lesson will have been learned, and these future problems recognized earlier and nipped in the bud.

Lessons Learned
1. In complex family situations, problem ownership may belong to all the participants.
2. Emotion rules the waves – cool levelheaded discussions simply don't take place.
3. The Utian Strategy is not infallible – sometimes it just doesn't work! In that case, at least seek the services of a family counselor!

Chapter 3

Race and Politics

All of us, at one time or another, will face issues of discrimination, whether related to matters such as race, religion, sexual preference, gender or socio-economic. This discrimination need not be directly personal, but such matters have an unpleasant tendency to involve many people within the vicinity of the ugly event. I, myself, have been caught up in two very nasty situations, both of which have had major influences on my own life. Applying my Utian Strategy was a challenge.

Personal Experience – South Africa's Apartheid

Some background is necessary for this story. Alan Paton described so well the background to South Africa in "Cry the Beloved Country." The book was written in 1947, published in 1948, the year in which the Afrikaner Nationalist Party swept into power and racial divide became institutionalized.

It was not until 1953 that the Nationalist Party, at the next election, was able to rig the ballot and bring into office a majority of two thirds of the seats in Parliament. This gave them free reign to change the so-called entrenched clauses of the constitution, South Africa's version of a bill of rights. Non-white voters were removed from the voters roll, and new acts like the Mixed Marriage Act (that is forbidding interracial marriage under penalty of law), the Group Areas Act (black poorly supported areas and white affluent suburbs) and the Education Act (separate but unequal) were brought into effect, all closely resembling the Nazi laws in Hitler's Germany.

I entered the Witwatersrand University Medical School in Johannesburg in 1957 as these acts were being enforced, and finished the six-year program in 1962. I completed my residency in obstetrics and gynecology at the University of Cape Town (UCT) and was appointed to the faculty in 1967. The government-controlled hospitals were already being segregated, although as a white physician, I was freely able to treat patients of all races in all hospitals, whether they were designated for white or non-white patients.

My non-white colleagues were not so fortunate, being restricted to treating patients only in those institutions approved for admitting non-white patients. Many of these individuals had been friends and classmates during my medical school years.

In 1970, I continued on the part-time staff of UCT and Groote Schuur Hospital, and started a private practice in obstetrics and gynecology. Success came rapidly. My offices were in central downtown Cape Town, and I made it a principle from day one that I saw all patients as they came, race never being an issue, and never asked when appointments were called in by telephone.

The ethics of medical practice in those days essentially meant that I was a consultant, and the bulk of my patients would be referred to me by general practitioners (GP) in the vicinity. Another professional practice was to invite the referring GP to assist at surgery, should an operation on their patient be necessary.

Sometime in mid-1973, by which time my practice had become one of the largest individual practices in the city, and I was working myself to death with 80-100 hour work weeks, delivering 30-40 babies per month as well as a heavy surgical schedule, an Asian-Indian GP colleague referred his 46-year-old sister-in-law for uncontrollable heavy vaginal bleeding with each of her periods. She had completed her family, was confirmed to have huge benign tumors of the uterus (uterine fibroids) and was clearly a candidate for hysterectomy. Following appropriate discussion and counseling, including consultation with her referring GP, we all agreed that hysterectomy would be undertaken. My nurse arranged admission to a local hospital accepting Asian-Indian patients, who in those days were classified as non-white, and the GP expressed his desire to assist at the procedure. Perhaps I should also mention that the Medical Superintendent (Super or MS) of such hospitals was essentially the senior administrator of the institution, a combination of Medical Director and CEO. The position at that time was always filled by a physician.

Several days later we were hard at it – scrubbed and busy in the operating room. The abdomen was open, the fibroids gigantic, and the procedure difficult. After completing one particularly intricate step in the surgery, I looked up to comment, and to my surprise and consternation, a complete stranger looked back at me. "Where is Dr. X?" I asked. "I'm not certain" was the response. "So who are you?" "I am the surgical resident" was the response from the young white male resident continuing "the medical super asked me to take your assistant's place when he called him out of the operating room."

Confused and concerned, I successfully completed the procedure, confirmed the patient was recovering well from anesthesia, and stepped out into the hallway. Standing there looking sheepish and embarrassed, dressed in his regular clothes, was my GP colleague. "What happened?" I asked. "The medical superintendent called me out and said it was against the law for me to be in the operating room." "Why?" – I responded, but he looked deflated, dispirited, obviously was deeply hurt and insulted, and did not want to discuss the matter. So after we had checked on the patient he left. I assured him he would hear further from me.

At this point, I was clueless as to what the problem was, never mind the ownership. But clearly my GP colleague was not the owner of the problem, and until I could learn more, it was all mine.

I stormed down to the medical superintendent's office, knocked on the door, entered his office, looked him in the eye, and asked what was going on. "You should know better!" he responded. "Should know what better?" "You cannot bring a non-white doctor into the operating room" he yelled. "What are you talking about? The patient was his sister-in-law and also Asian-Indian!" "The scrub nurse was white, and we can't have any non-white doctor giving orders to white nurses. Anyway, we don't have toilets here for these people!" "For God's sake, he wasn't looking for the toilet, he was assisting me in the operating room! You interfered directly in care of my patient in the middle of an operating procedure and I promise you this is not the last you will hear of this!"

Angry, embarrassed, frustrated, determined to get retribution, I stormed out as I had stormed in.

At this point, there were a number of factors that I had to consider:

1. The problem was not mine; it had been nurtured by the Apartheid system, but initiated by the MS. He owned the problem.

2. In Apartheid South Africa, I did not have a lot of recourse I could consider. If I had taken this to government appointed hospital authorities, they would have thrown me out.

3. Already, arrest without charges, holding of people for 90-180 days without lawyers, trumped up charges and worse were the order of the day. There was an element of personal risk to challenging the system.

4. I was not the injured party. My GP colleague was the victim, and his desires had to be taken into account.

5. I needed to be cautious in approach and should seek counsel from medical colleagues, probably through our medical organization, the South African Medical Association.

I was a young Turk in those days, deeply committed to "principles" when it came to conflict, and my father's son, always remembering his explaining his own direct approach to conflict resolution "what is on my lung is on my tongue." Speaking out too quickly, sometimes without carefully considering all the issues, frequently got him deeper into problems than before, and certainly the same has happened to me.

Above all, I was angry and offended and was going to do something.

So at this point, while not the owner of the problem, I had chosen ownership of the problem because I intended to turn it around, deliver it back to the MS and seek an apology for my GP colleague.

I called several friends on the Executive Committee of the local branch of the South African Medical Association (SAMA). All basically gave the same response, look you are right, but there is nothing to be gained by taking it further, you will only compromise your advance in the health system, and may, even worse, put your personal safety at risk. I called my GP colleague who had suffered the insult and he told me "you can do what you like, but I won't do anything myself. I don't want things worse for me. You go right ahead if you want to." I read into his words a high desire for me to do something, but low expectation that in fact I would.

My options were limited. How do you take a complication of a systemic problem directly back into that system to get some positive resolution? Speaking again to the MS was useless – he was inefficient, pompous, arrogant, lacked insight, and believed that the Bible confirmed that he was right.

In South Africa all practitioners were registered and licensed to practice by the South African Medical Council (SAMC), a government appointed agency. There was a code of ethics, amongst which was the pattern of behavior between colleagues and interaction with patients. I chose to challenge the system through a smoke screen of medical ethics. This entailed submitting a formal complaint to the SAMC that the offending MS had directly interfered in the care of my patient during intricate surgery with no valid reason. I further complained that the race issue did not exist, as the patient was the same race as the GP and he was not giving the orders to the nurse as I was the surgeon. I requested the MS have his medical license revoked, be disbarred from practice, and hence fired from his job.

Duly lodged, I awaited a response. Imagine my surprise and disappointment when the response came not from the government agency (SAMC) but from one of the senior officers of our professional organization (SAMA). "Look Wulf" he said, in summary, "these things happen, there is little to be gained by making an issue of it. Nothing will be done; this is the system we all accept by living in it and working in it. I have also been asked by my colleagues to implore you to withdraw your letter before it reaches public knowledge (the media). As you know, there is an upcoming meeting of the Commonwealth Medical Association in London, England. Already they are threatening South Africa and the South African Medical Association that because of our acceptance of Apartheid, we will be disbarred and expelled from the commonwealth organization. If this hits the newspapers, then that will be the last chance for us to stay in the association. Just accept it!"

Now it was obvious to me that my own colleagues were not only accepting the status quo, but were attempting to transfer ownership of an even bigger problem which was the response of the South African Medical Association to the very policy of Apartheid. Suddenly, South Africa's continued medical status in international politics was my problem, the guilt factor being used as the transference tool.

Worse! He continued, "Wulf, I should also tell you that there is some rumor that your family could be at personal danger and your house firebombed!"

Not only guilt as a weapon, but fear as well! It was shortly after that we realized our phone line was being tapped – with no attempt whatsoever to disguise the fact.

Then the issue exploded. The story came to the attention of the world media. I never learned who leaked it, but always suspected that it was one of the nurses at the hospital who herself had been pretty disgusted by the whole thing.

A full-page headline in the Sunday Times of Johannesburg, July 29, 1973 read "Operating Theatre Drama" with the subheading "Indian Doctor Ordered Out After Objections." The full details of the story were described. Within a short time, the news was worldwide. For example, the Observer of London on July 29, 1973 placed an article headed "Nurse Had Dr. Put Out."

This example of a major problem does serve a valuable lesson. Under situations of extreme like this, although you are not responsible for the origin of the problem, do you accept the ball, or do you drop it, or do you throw it back?

For myself, many sleepless nights made me realize that if I ignored the situation, then I would be guilty by association. I could not live with myself. The system was rotten – the solution for me for that problem was to start making plans to get the hell out of it. Thus, I had recognized that this problem actually had several elements – including the core issue at the hospital, but in addition the fact that I was living in an unhealthy political environment.

Clearly recognizing these elements, I decided to:

1. Continue to fight – accept the problem – demand the cancellation of the medical license of the offending MS – or have the system agree they were wrong.

2. Start making undercover plans to move my family out of South Africa, despite the fact that I had reached a satisfying peak in my career, this was home, and everything we possessed was around us.

The resolution of the first decision was remarkably rapid. I believe the media pressure was too great. In my favor was the fact that the Provincial Government of the Cape Province was far more liberal than the Pretoria dominated Central Government.

Out of the blue, I received a call from the Director of Medical Affairs of the Cape Provincial Government. He asked if I was persisting in my complaint. I affirmed I was. He asked if I would consider dropping the charges in return for a personal apology to myself and the GP from the hospital MS in his presence and a new law proposed that non-white physicians could assist white physicians in surgery.

This was a real surprise, obviously not perfect, but progress nonetheless. I thanked him and informed him that I would confer with my GP colleague and call him back. The GP was astonished, agreed this was more than expected, that we should accept the terms. That day, in the Cape Minister of Health's Office, the apology was grudgingly offered to the two of us by the hospital medical superintendent in the presence of the Minister of Health. Shortly thereafter, in the Cape Argus, Cape Town's major evening newspaper, a major headline appeared announcing "Provision Being Made" and sub-heading "Facilities for Non-White Cape Doctors."

I had won the battle, but in my heart of hearts, knew I had lost the war. If I ever desired an advanced academic position in medicine, I should look beyond the South African borders.

My second decision took longer, and some time after putting out the necessary feelers, I received a call from Cleveland, Ohio (from where?). Brian Little, the Chairman of Obstetrics and Gynecology at Case Western Reserve University was inviting me to a six-month Sabbatical in his department. We accepted, moved to the USA, and 44 years later I joke that I am still on Sabbatical.

Lessons Learned

1. Sometimes you have no alternative but to accept ownership of someone else's problem. But when you do so, you go in with eyes wide open. Know what you are accepting.

2. Recognize the elements of the problem, and in strategizing a solution, work towards the best possible outcome for those elements – the result may not be perfect, but they should at least be acceptable.

3. Maintain a high level of alertness for all innuendos, use of language, including body language.

4. Be certain that people you think are on your side really are.

Personal Experience – The Race Weapon In America

Barely seven years later, in 1980 to be exact, I came face to face with a racial divide issue in Cleveland that made me wonder whether I had jumped from the frying pan into the fire. Race issues are not limited to racially divided dictatorships.

Again, this is an involved story, but it too offers a lesson in problem identification, recognition of ownership, and strategy for resolution. In this instance, a little luck also helped, but doesn't it always, if one should only be so lucky! Cleveland was a shock to the system. In 1976, it looked like a city in self-destruct, with areas resembling cities I had seen in the 60's with residual damage following the second World War in Europe. In the recent past, the river had caught fire, so too had the Mayor's hair burned! The inner city indeed looked like Berlin after World War II.

The University Circle area of Cleveland was one of its few redeeming features. It contained multiple museums and institutions – the respected Cleveland Museum of Art, the world-renowned Cleveland Orchestra, and big hospitals like University Hospitals of Cleveland and the Cleveland Clinic. Also contained is the campus of Case Western Reserve University, the medical school having its primary affiliation with University Hospitals, but other teaching hospitals as well, like The Mt. Sinai Medical Center.

Today, Cleveland is a medical megalopolis – nothing in the world of medicine happens if it isn't also happening in Cleveland. Then, some of the hospitals were pretty derelict. Mt. Sinai Medical Center was as derelict as any, but in the late 1970's, a new Board of Directors had raised money and had plans for a big hospital turn around that was to include expanded staff and building a major new wing to the hospital. Part of that revival was the appointment of a full-time director of obstetrics and gynecology, and I was invited to consider the position. To this day, other than that they agreed to fund an In Vitro Fertilization laboratory (and that was 1979 just as the world was learning of the concept with the birth of Louise Brown in England), I do not know why I stayed in Cleveland and accepted the challenge – most likely just inertia.

Between 1976 and 1979, I had developed a friendship with one of my reproductive endocrinology fellows at University Hospitals, and had also secured a high-risk obstetrics fellowship position there for a former Cape Town resident of mine. We all three decided to team up and assume the challenge of converting a derelict department of OB/GYN into a center of excellence.

We found a department comprising one secretary sitting in a dingy office, filled floor to ceiling with dusty old files, and eight residents, two in each of the four years of the program. As I recall, they were the sorriest bunch of individuals I had ever encountered in an academic institution. I also inherited a large group of part-time staff who had their private practices in the city or suburbs and admitted patients to the hospital, but that is another lesson for later. Let me first give the story about the residents in training.

Within a short while it became obvious to us that three of these residents were probably the most poorly trained, non-motivated, incompetent individuals we had ever encountered, in short, a potential menace to their patients. Months of counseling, education, instruction and motivation provided no resolution. They were as bad as ever, and patient care was at risk.

So here I was, relatively new in the country, this being my fourth year in Cleveland and the USA, having just assumed a position of responsibility that was clearly riddled with problems, and facing my first crucial test. What do I do?

Analysis

1. The medical resident program was in trouble, particularly because three of the eight residents were a problem.
2. By assuming directorship of the department, I had accepted ownership of the problem.
3. The residents themselves could not recognize that they were a problem.
4. Education and encouragement were not resolving the problem.

5. Health care delivery and quality was being severely jeopardized

In this instance, I did not need to be a rocket scientist to recognize the solution – they should find a different area of medical specialization as far away as possible from OB/GYN.

I fired them with due process; one was a white Jewish male, one an Asian-Indian male, and the third an African-American female. They all left; but the African-American woman sued me for racism and sexism. I was astounded. Worse, she hired as her attorney, the all-powerful African-American Chairman of the Cleveland City Council, known for his use of power and position. Me! Me, who had left South Africa largely because of my support for racial equality, was being sued for racism by an African-American female!

Analysis
I had a big problem, and this problem was mine!

The course of events, which I assure you are true, will read like a novel. The hospital promised to back me all the way, that is until they began to feel the pressure.

Within a week of the suit being lodged, I was called into the first of many crisis meetings in the office of the hospital CEO. Also present, as I recall, were the chief of staff, the hospital legal representative and a Board member. I was informed that they had heard the opposition planned to be aggressive in their suit and that within the next couple of days, unless I rehired the woman, they were calling a press conference to announce that Mt. Sinai Medical Center had hired an apartheid-racist white South African male, one of whose first actions was to fire an innocent African-American female physician. Accordingly, they would be proceeding with a suit against me and the hospital with charges of racism and sexism.

I was appalled. The incongruity was altogether a nightmare.

Analysis
1. My problem was getting worse.
2. It was also the hospital's problem.
3. The only approaches were to maintain the course, or accept defeat and take her back.
4. I was encountering a new form of bully tactic I had never previously experienced.

Accordingly, I discussed these options with the participants in the CEO's meeting. I emphasized that what I was doing was morally correct, in the patients' best interest, and the reason that they had hired me was to improve patient care. Therefore, I intended to hold to my decision. I also requested the attorney to advise the opposite camp that I too would call a press conference, report the Cleveland Council Chairman's lack of concern for the quality of health care delivered to the inner city population, and wondered how the media would react to the news that a white South African male was suing an African-American female on the basis of defamation of character and racism.

They never called their press conference. Neither did I. But the battle was obviously going to be nasty. The Board approved plan for building a new wing and renovating the hospital was moving right along. Part of the site for the new hospital building involved a small piece of derelict sidewalk that was owned by the Cleveland City Council. The City

Council had previously agreed to gift this parcel of land to Mt. Sinai Medical Center for the new building, the hospital providing most of the emergency medical care for the inner-city population.

To the surprise of all concerned at the hospital, shortly after the press conference threat had seemed to abate, the hospital received a letter from the Cleveland City Council advising that usage of that piece of land needed approval from a special committee of the city's Parks Department before building could commence. I wish you could have seen the small derelict piece of territory. A couple of days later, the hospital chief of staff, a fine individual, approached me and said they had heard from the town councilman/lawyer in an unrecorded conversation that if I would take the resident back, the issue of the parcel of land could be rapidly expedited through the Parks Department and building could commence.

Next thing, I received a personal visit from the chairman of the hospital Board. He invited me for a walk, during which time he informed me that I was "a newcomer to these fair shores of the United States and things were generally done different to most other places. I needed to learn the art of compromise. Take her back for a year, keep a record of all the new problems, then you'll have a better case if you still need to get rid of her". "You know", I responded "I really understand the score. You want this new hospital built. You want your name for posterity on the foundation stone. As for me, I have worked in some pretty old buildings in my career. The four walls are not the standard of care; it's the people who work between them and administer the care that count. For me, I can be perfectly satisfied with the old buildings. The case goes on!"

Analysis
1. The hospital is buckling – they're making their problem mine.
2. My position is getting precarious.
3. The weapon of guilt was being used to force compliance.
4. I now no longer could rely on the Board for support.

Proof came sooner than I expected. I was due to leave one afternoon for a medical conference in Europe. When I entered the hospital parking garage early that morning, the attendant at the entrance waved me down and said the hospital CEO needed to see me in his office immediately. I parked, dropped my briefcase in my office, and went downstairs.

The war council was in full session. Present in the room were the hospital CEO, the chairman of the Board, the chief of staff, and the lawyers. The CEO launched straight into it – "They have offered a final compromise settlement. The woman comes back for a six-month probationary period during which time she will be carefully monitored by three of the part-time staff, but not by you or your two full-time colleagues. If she errs, she leaves. If not, she stays. We, all of us in our official capacity, are recommending *("insisting?")* that you accept."

"You mean that all the remaining residents in the program and the entire hospital staff will know that I, as Director, and my full-time colleagues, will have no say in the judgment of standards of practice of one of my residents?"

"That's about the extent of it."

Analysis:

I am being given an ultimatum, accept our problem and really make it yours.

My mind had been working at double speed, so it did not take long for me to deliver my response "I really do understand the situation. The whole hospital development has been put on hold because of an issue involving one resident in one department. For the good of the whole, there needs to be compromise by one of the parts. Okay. I agree. You can have the resident, you can have the new hospital building, and you can have my resignation. Good day. I am leaving for Europe!"

I left them, all staring at me in surprise.

Halfway down the hallway back to my office, the chief of staff caught up with me. "Wulf, there is worse. We have reason to believe there is a credible threat that your house might be firebombed. The hospital is willing to put Moira and the kids up at the Marriott while you are away."

Incredibly, almost the identical words I had heard in apartheid South Africa in 1973 were being repeated to me in Cleveland, Ohio in 1980.

Analysis:

Now the weapon of fear was being added – accept the problem as well as their solution.

I called Moira and said there is bad news (I have resigned) and worse news (the threat of a firebomb). Moira's brave response – we can go to plenty of other places; they will never firebomb us; this is 1980 in America.

She stayed home and I went to Europe – feelings of anxiety and guilt following me. I had made my problem my family's problem.

A few days later I returned to Cleveland, confirmed all was well at home, and went to the hospital planning to start clearing out my office. I was met in the hallway by the chief of staff, his face beaming in a broad smile. His wife was an anesthetist on the staff of The Cleveland Clinic. While I was away, she had unearthed a file that documented that our female resident had previously been employed at The Cleveland Clinic Foundation (CCF), had been fired for incompetence, had sued the CCF for racism and sexism, and had lost her case. Her subsequent application forms to our hospital had been falsified and showed no reference to the CCF events. Her attorney had been notified that unless he withdrew the case, the hospital would call a press conference and disclose all the facts including the stalling of the new hospital development.

The case was withdrawn. I still had a job. The news spread like wildfire through the hospital. My first step was to ask my secretary to call an emergency meeting of all my residents. "You have all heard the news. From now on, you will all wash, wear clean clothes, perform your duties 100% and hit the books hard. Otherwise, you are next." From that day onwards, the residents called me "sir", and the program improved beyond belief.

Final Analysis
1. Have principles and stick to them.
2. Don't let anyone force ownership of their problems on you.
3. Luck helps, but don't rely on it

Chapter 4

The Workplace

The Utian Strategy for problem recognition and ownership has few incubators of need as great as the workplace. It is an unfortunate truth that the larger the hierarchy, the more likely it will be that problems developed at an upper level will be "gifted" to someone of lower rank. Remember the Peter Principle, "In every hierarchy, every employee rises to his/her level of incompetence." Small businesses are less likely to be affected, but are not immune from this. Peter's description of the outstanding schoolteacher with 20 years' experience (actually one year's experience 20 times) who is promoted to school principal well illustrates his theory. Absolutely untrained in management, this would be the exact individual to initiate problems, fail to recognize problems, or, most certainly, to transfer ownership to some poor teacher down the hierarchy.

Managers, business owners, CEOs, department directors, and indeed anyone with a position of responsibility, when assuming office is faced with an immediate problem - how to recognize the dead wood, the incompetent, the inefficient, the lazy, and, worst of all, the employee with no insight.

This situation is one of inherited ownership of existing problems – by accepting the promotion or new appointment, you are accepting all existing problems and assuming the responsibility of resolving them. That is why you are hired, implicit in the contract.

Case History: Cleaning House

Another problem I inherited on assuming the directorship of the department of OB/GYN at Mt. Sinai Medical Center was that of a very complex part-time staff. These were private practicing OB/GYN's with offices away from the hospital in the city or in the suburbs, but who admitted patients to the hospital. For years, with minimal oversight or quality assurance, they had developed a disparate set of practices. Some were well trained, practiced quality medicine, and worked well in training the residents. Others, well, at best, their practice patterns were questionable. Some worked in solo practice, some functioned in groups. In essence, they were competitors, but with a new department director in place, me, they could certainly all agree on one thing. At the very least, our new team was a nuisance.

Analysis

1. The fundamental problem was that several physicians appeared to be practicing below current acceptable standards.
2. The problem was mine to rxesolve.
3. The offenders needed to be identified through review of specific cases.
4. Standards of practice and better care pathways needed to be developed.
5. A mechanism for risk management, problem identification and quality assurance had to be put into effect.
6. I would need the support of the quality physicians.

The strategy developed to achieve success involved a combination of problem awareness and transference using teamwork and collegiality. That is, working with my two full-time colleagues, we essentially itemized the medical conditions with poor outcomes. Then, through a series of educational meetings, largely what the medical community calls "grand rounds", where an outside expert on the subject comes in to lecture to the department, we made the physicians recognize specific issues of concern. Following this conscience raising awareness strategy, we would develop and circulate a set of practice guidelines, defining what would be "best practice of medicine."

It was around this time that myself and two colleagues, comprising the "full-time staff," recognized that we had to try and reduce the tension between the "them and us" - the town gown phenomenon. This was never to be easy. But we strategized that if my colleagues could be seen as collegial, impacted equally by the new practice guidelines, there might be a reduction in tension. In essence, they were to become "messengers" rather than "supervisors." This of course meant we had consciously embarked on a good cop/bad cop approach. They were to be the nice guys – "look, this is what Wulf wants in place to improve patient care, and it affects our clinical practice as much as yours." Unfortunately, their being nice guys meant I was to become the bad guy. They would offer the carrot and I would wield the stick. I had never played such a role before, but the strategy worked, and in the process I developed a reputation of being a tough guy. This certainly did not win me friends, but I was not in the job for a social life.

Lesson

1. Problems can be identified, and the offending party made aware of them by indirect non-offensive approaches.
2. Partial transference of ownership can be achieved without any direct discussion.
3. A team approach to resolving problems simplifies the process.

The strategy worked, and our new OB/GYN department flourished.

In the process, specific physicians with specific problems were exposed. The most difficult example concerned two elderly gynecologists, one about 89 and the other 93 years old and both still performing surgery! So bad was the situation, the residents would compete not to assist at surgery; when they did, they would order double the number of units of blood for re-transfusion than any good surgeon would possibly require. Surgery was sometimes described as a blood bath.

Analysis

1. The problem was two over the hill surgeons insisting on operating and putting patients at risk.
2. I was the new department director – although the problem in essence was theirs, I had assumed ownership.
3. There was no mandatory retirement age for medical practice in the institution or the State of Ohio.
4. I needed to identify specific cases with bad outcomes, and then in a sensitive manner, withdraw their surgical privileges.

In a short time new but similar problem were identified, and I had to steel myself to have private separate chats with these MD's. The 93-year-old was only too pleased to stop practicing. The 89-year-old was offended and threatened to fight me to the bitter end. And so he did. But he fouled up; this was observed directly by one of the proctor's I had put in place. The result of the process led to termination of his surgical privileges and the patients were spared.

Resolving this problem did not entirely take the situation off my shoulders – for several years thereafter he would call me at home late at night and scream over the phone "you destroyed my medical career!" Win some, lose some!

Case History – The CEO Without Insight

Several years of hard work, with pioneering techniques in infertility treatment and menopause management, led to rapid growth in the department. A rising tide lifts all ships, and the part-time practitioners affiliated with Mt. Sinai Medical Center enjoyed unprecedented practice growth as the hospital developed the reputation for the place to be for excellent quality care.

But I and my colleagues were working beyond endurance and needed help. Our contracts were also up and due for re-negotiation. During those years, the hospital Chief Executive Officer (CEO) had changed. The original CEO whose handshake was his word was replaced by a classic bureaucrat. Negotiations with him were a nightmare. I explained that we needed to employ additional full-time staff as the full-time department practice volume increased. By that time, we were getting infertility patients from far and wide, having initiated one of the first successful In

Vitro Fertilization centers in the world, and conducting training courses for doctors all over the world in current treatments for infertility.

"What you don't understand Wulf, is that I need the part-time private practitioners to admit patients and fill the beds. They see you as competitors and it would be threatening to them if I allowed you to expand." Poor little Mt. Sinai Medical Center tucked between the giants, the Cleveland Clinic (CCF) and University Hospitals of Cleveland (UHC), and we were being seen as the competition!

I tried to respond to him. "What you don't understand, is that by enhancing the reputation of this medical center, we have helped the part-timers grow their practices. Remember a rising tide lifts all ships. We aren't the competition, the CCF and UHC are the competition!"

He just did not get it.

Analysis

1. We owned the problem – we were victims of our own success – we were overworked and needed help.
2. The hospital CEO had a problem, fear of offending the part-time practitioners.
3. He would not recognize our problem.
4. He was trying to make his problem, our problem.

So, what to do?

Options

1. Accept the situation and work harder.
2. Seek an alternate option.

Luck played into my hands. The previous academic chairman of the OB/GYN department at University Hospitals and Case Western Reserve University (CWRU) had resigned in the previous year. I was approached by the University Hospitals CEO and the Dean at the CWRU Medical School inviting me to apply for the position. I did, and informed The Mt. Sinai Medical Center's CEO, who was furious.

Analysis
He had a new problem.

1. Worse, he was not aware of exactly of what his problem was.
2. I had spent a decade building The Mt. Sinai Medical Center department and wanted it to continue to be successful – of course, that was my problem.

As I worked with the Dean of CWRU School of Medicine and the CEO of UH defining my new departmental terms and personal package, I advised them of my desire that the MSMC not be harmed in the process of my transfer. The Dean, particularly as MSMC was a CWRU affiliate, was interested in some sort of co-relationship between the MSMC and UH departments. The CEO of MSMC was not. At that time the MSMC was beginning to struggle, even facing potential closure, and I suggested an imaginative new approach. The physical space at UH for women and children's care was limited and in need of expensive reconstruction. What about converting the MSMC hospital into the MSMC/UH Women's and Children's Hospital, saving the future existence of the MSMC at the same time as opening up much-needed space for expansion of other medical services on the UH campus? The CEO of MSMC angrily rejected the idea.

Analysis
1. One problem can sometimes be replaced by another.
2. Ownership of a problem can swing from party to party like a tennis ball.
3. It is possible to lose sight of the precise problem – the MSMC CEO was certainly doing that.

My full-time faculty moved with me across to UHC/CWRU School of Medicine. Over the next decade, that department once again became one of the top academic and clinical departments in the USA. The MSMC department? It never recovered from the loss of its full-time OB/GYN faculty, and despite several attempts to fill the slots, the department gradually sunk into oblivion. As for the CEO, well, be careful of what you wish for. He certainly did not understand the strategy of problem recognition and solving. His mind was on a non-existent problem. In essence, he fiddled while MSMC burned, and soon after, the Hospital was closed permanently. Today, most of it is a parking lot.

Lesson
Keep your eye on the ball! Always be aware of the precise nature of the problem, recognizing where ownership resides. Watch out for subplots that can intrude along the way.

Case History – The Difficult and Aggressive Manager
Not all work problems are confined to large organizations. A particularly striking example of problem management occurred in a business of just eight employees.

Background

Barely six weeks before departing MSMC for CWRU into the role of academic chairman and directorship of the UHC clinical department, I founded a not-for-profit organization called The North American Menopause Society (NAMS). My new administrative secretary was already in place at University Hospitals, and, showing her a stack of about 20 manila folders, explained what I had done. I asked if she would be prepared to work with me on the organization. "I am confident it will take less than 15 minutes of your time per week." Actually, within a few years, she had given up her job at UH and became the full-time administrative director of an organization that now has more than 2,000 members in over 50 countries, multiple publications, huge annual scientific meetings, and numerous projects constantly in progress.

Truly this was a success story, the extent of which was unexpected, but obviously gratifying. But rapid development can bring problems in its wake. The growth was necessarily paralleled by staff acquisition and by 2003 there were eight employees in an active organizational office. The staff was essentially divided into me as Executive Director, two organizational directors; one administrative and one for education and development, and the rest. The lesson on problem resolution occurred between the Education Director and one of the staff working on consumer education materials. Both were women in their early 50's.

I think it would not be unfair to describe them both. The education director, we will call her Norma, was an extremely hardworking, diligent, highly intelligent, and highly motivated individual, obsessive in her search for perfection. Her one weakness was an absolute intolerance for anything that did not meet her standards, and, although almost always of a friendly and smiling disposition, she occasionally had an extremely short fuse and could erupt in anger. The employee was a mature, responsible, capable, diligent, meticulous individual who was soft-spoken and generally of even disposition. We will call her Alice.

From multiple experiences over several years, I was aware that the Educational Director could erupt into anger, upsetting an employee, and had counseled her several times. Once aware of the problem, she always cooled down for a while.

The incident in question probably resulted from some minor mistake. Norma exploded, insinuating that Alice was incompetent, not working as efficiently as she should and so on. Alice arrived in my office in tears, described the incident, telling me that this had happened several times, she could not tolerate it, no one had the right to speak to her that way and if I couldn't do something to correct the problem, she would have no alternative but to resign.

Summary

1. There was a manager/employee personality problem.
2. The actual issue over which the conflict occurred was small and irrelevant.
3. The manager was subject to fits of temper; the employee was feeling unable to handle it.

Questions

1. Whose problem was it?
2. Was there more than one problem?

Analysis
1. There are two problems.
2. Problem #1 – fits of anger – belongs to Norma.
3. Problem #2 – difficult in handling an angry manager belongs to Alice.
4. Less than subtly, they were transferring their problems to me.
5. It could also be argued that I have a problem, handling an employee with a problem, anger.

Action
Once I had Alice calmed down, I explained my analysis to her and gave her options for follow-up. Alice's options:

1. She should accept ownership of her problem and deal with it. For example, she could make an appointment with Norma and suggest that her anger and overreaction was over the top, and really not acceptable.
2. She should request that I assume her problem and speak for her, but that would not do much for her own self-image and respect.

Alice asked me to speak to Norma, but to wait a day or two while she thought things over.

Two days later she came into my office, said she was accepting ownership of the problem and would like to deal with it in her own time. Knowing I was available in the background was a reassurance, but she had made an appointment with a counselor to get help.

About 10 days went by before I saw Alice again in my office. "Counseling was a great help. I have spoken with Norma and have told her that I am a mature adult and she has no right to speak to me the way she did. To my surprise, Norma apologized and said I was right. You have no idea how good I feel about myself and my future in the job!"

Comment

The preceding case history is an excellent example of someone who brought face-to-face with problem analysis and ownership, accepted the message, ran with it, solved her own problem, and reaped the rewards.

Day-To-Day Application of the Strategy

From the time I became a medical department director, I put The Utian Strategy to work in personnel management. With all the changes, diverse personalities, internal/external conflicts, and day-to-day issues, it was clear that I could be inundated with problems. This is a choice facing any manager – become a micromanager and assume all the problems (the great example of course was when Jimmy Carter was President of the USA and insisted on taking control of reserving times for the White House tennis court), or be a macro manager, give employees space to develop, and grow the whole organization.

Without thinking twice, I chose the latter, and so advised my staff at an early business meeting, "I am going to give you plenty of rope. While I am going to be incredibly generous on the one hand, the other hand will be waiting for you to deliver. Your career growth and development enhances my success as a director, but if problems come in my door, we will need to meet, and I cannot promise a pleasant discussion!"

I also announced an open-door policy. My office door would stand open at all times for anyone to approach me.

My strategy of course was to encourage progress of the department through the growth of the individuals. They were to deal with their division problems. Department problems would be mine.

What this meant was that whenever anyone entered my office and asked if they could discuss an issue with me, I was only too pleased to say "sure, come in, sit down, tell me what's up."

Then I would listen very carefully.

The question foremost in my mind while I was listening – is this my problem, or is this your problem?

Follow-up discussion would always run the same course. In every instance, I would attempt to dissect the problem to its core elements – "as I understand it, the problem is (and I would define it). Do I understand the situation correctly?"

Beyond that, the conversation would proceed in one of two directions –

1. EITHER: "You know, as I read things, this is your problem. Go away, think about it, and plan on how you intend to resolve it. Then, just do it. Let me know the outcome."

2. OR: "Yes, clearly this is my problem. Leave it with me. I will work things out and let you know the outcome."

In simple terms, I was educating my staff and colleagues to recognize that problem ownership is integral to problem resolution. I was not allowing anyone else to transfer problem ownership to me and hence to make departmental management more difficult if not impossible.

The Message to Remember!

Next time someone approaches you with – "there is a problem. . ." – try this approach, and see how well it works. Ask yourself, is this my problem or is this your problem?

Chapter 5

Health and Healthcare

I have spent my entire adult life in healthcare delivery, observing it from every perspective, as practicing physician, hospital department director, practice manager, university academic department chairman, researcher, administrator, founder of professional organizations, and as a real learning experience being a patient myself.

The more I am involved, the more confusing the whole system appears to be. Of course, systems vary country by country. In the USA, they even vary state-by-state, region-by-region, and city-by-city. Different patterns of medical practice all complicate the matter, with different outcomes for the same disease, different insurance and reimbursement systems, and two or three tier health systems, those for the poor and disadvantaged, verse the average citizen, verse the upper affluent or influential privileged few.

Patients going through a severe health issue with hospitalization can inherit a paper avalanche that needs an MBA to understand.

Our complex health system has been turned into each and every citizen's problem. In short, the system has made its problem, our problem.

For illustration, I am going to address health-related problems from three perspectives:

1. Dealing with personal health issues.
2. Accessing healthcare and dealing with the system.
3. Being the caregiver for someone with serious problems.

Let's go through each of these issues one by one.

1. Personal Health Issues

Inevitably, every one of us is going to face the prospect of a serious medical diagnosis. Sometimes the news will creep in slowly – an increasing pain, developing shortness of breath, gradual increasing intensity of headaches – and following some testing, the diagnosis will be given – heart disease, obstructive lung disease, diabetes, cancer, and so on. Sometimes the blow comes suddenly – heart attack, stroke, or fractured hip.

Each disease has its specific features, risks and outcomes. All have some features in common. All raise issues beyond the disease itself – how long will I live, do I need to make some arrangement to finalize my estate, what will happen to my spouse and family, what to do with the business?

Summary

1. Disease hits – slowly or suddenly.
2. Personal adjustments need to be made in coping with the effect of the disease and dealing with the knowledge that life is fragile.
3. Healthcare is needed – this will be discussed below.
4. Contemporary medicine places a responsibility of ensuring health and dealing with disease directly on the affected individual.

5. More has to be learned about the disease itself – its natural history, options for treatment, best doctors and hospitals, etc.
6. Personal affairs need to be set in order.
7. Communicating with family and friends can be complex.

Above All, You Need to Recognize That It Is You with the Disease – It Is First and Foremost Your Problem.

All of the above seems fairly obvious. Yet, many has been a time in my clinical practice that the patient has practiced denial, become immobile with fear, immediately look to me to make the therapeutic decisions for her or pass all the decision-making issues on to her husband, son or daughter.

Years ago, when I first was a medical student and in my early practice years, the diagnosis of cancer became a family charade. No one, doctor or family, mouthed the word cancer to the patient, everything was kept secret, and the family accepted all the recommendations of Professor Herr Doktor!

Today, the pendulum has swung completely to the other side. The patient is immediately informed, the outcomes and potential complications explained in cruel detail, the patient instructed that all decision-making is hers. Every doctor practices with a litigation lawyer on the shoulder – dozens of tests, necessary or not, are undertaken. Indeed, invariably, more attention is given to ensuring a perfect office or hospital record than to the patient herself.

These are only a few of the problems in the current system for health delivery – and a topic for a separate book in itself.

Simply put, severe disease brings with it a heavy burden of both medical decision-making and non-disease related problems to deal with.

A Personal Story

There are times when my problem can immediately be your problem as well. My extreme example is one experience I wish I had not needed to relate since much of it involves a personal nightmare. A routine annual check-up revealed a slightly elevated prostate specific antigen (PSA) level, which led to a prostate biopsy on a Wednesday late in September 2003. The urologist was out of town for the next two days, precluding my getting biopsy results quickly. My wife Moira and I celebrated our 39th wedding anniversary on Saturday, October 4th. Our son was in town and, after dinner, the three of us went to a movie. Coincidence of coincidence: my urologist and his wife happened to be sitting next to us. After a perceptible silence, he leaned over my family and asked me to join him in the lobby, where he bluntly informed me that I had prostate cancer. After a few moments alone in deep thought, I re-entered the theater. My wife was ashen. We looked into each other's eyes, I nodded, and she burst into tears. My son sat in silent shock.

My mind immediately split into a multiple personality mode. The "personal mind" suddenly questioned my mortality; the "medical mind" reviewed the potential management implications; the "practical mind" deliberated the important projects and international meetings I was committed to in the near future. But the "professional physician mind" observed the instant reactions of my wife and my son, and I was forcibly struck by the medical implications of this diagnosis on the spouse or significant other.

In essence, I had been presented with a problem, and although it was mine, it clearly was also an immediate problem for my wife and family.

Prostate cancer is a leading cause of illness and death among men. While about one in nine women will have developed breast cancer by the time they're in their early 80s, autopsy series have revealed prostate cancer to be present in 64% of men between the ages of 60 and 70. About 1 man in 41 will die of prostate cancer, only second to deaths from lung cancer. Deaths due to prostate cancer in the U.S. almost equal the number of women who die from breast cancer. The scary facts are that in 2019 0ver 24 per cent of cancer deaths in males were because of prostate cancer and 37 per cent of cancer deaths in women were because of breast cancer. Worldwide, about 1.2 million men were diagnosed with prostate cancer in 2018 (International Agency for Research on Cancer, 2019). The US is expected to have the highest number of diagnosed incident cases, increasing from 170,744 cases in 2018 to 204,127 cases in 2028.

Some of the numbers are the outcome of women living longer than men, on average. Simply put, it is far more likely that women will have a male partner with prostate cancer, than men have a partner with breast cancer.

But this is not a review of prostate cancer; it is a call to recognize that the diagnosis of any major disease has an impact on the life of the spouse/partner that is almost as severe as the impact on the individual who has been diagnosed. With prostate cancer as an example, there are just so many issues the woman faces with her partner in life: the shock of hearing the diagnosis, the concern and empathy for her friend and lover; the practicalities of decision-making regarding the treatment options of observation, surgery or radiotherapy; learning for the first time about potential complications, such as urinary incontinence, impotence, proctitis (rectal inflammation) or urethritis (bladder irritation); working through the immediate treatment process; loss, at least for a while, of a sexual partner; contemplating life and fear of death and dying; facing the prospect of living alone; the emotional ups and downs, the stress, the worry, the sleepless nights, and the self-doubt; the economic concerns and the impact on personal life and career.

Fortunately, there are also potential upsides. These include relief, if surgery is successful; joy, upon hearing that the pathology is localized; gradual return to a normal life; eventual resumption of sexual union; a new shared perspective on life; and the desire to take time out to "smell the roses." For the record, I have been extremely lucky, and have had a complete recovery.

These are only a few immediate concerns that demand attention. All of us will have to acquire some knowledge and understanding of the potential diseases that our partners or loved ones may develop. But more than that—far more than that—we need to develop and enhance skills to provide support, empathy, and understanding, in a direct effort to assist in lessening the burden, and to help them to cope with the situation to which they have suddenly been exposed. In turn, there is a problem not well addressed by health care providers – and that is providing the above services to the caregiver.

Women are more fortunate than men. They socialize better throughout their lives, bond more strongly to friends, share experiences more openly, and have a far more supportive network than do men.

Lesson Learned
1. Some problems can and should be co-owned.
2. Sharing the burden can ease the load!

How to Cope
1. Realize immediately it is your problem.
2. Seek all the help you can get.
3. Make your own decisions.
4. Don't second-guess once you have entered a specific treatment pathway.
5. Share personal thoughts and tender moments with your loved ones – but spare them the added pain of loading them with additional burdens or feelings of guilt.
6. Make use of all the contemporary healthcare to which you are entitled.

2. Accessing Health Care – Dealing with the System

We have a multi-tier healthcare system in the USA. Your level largely depends on your income. The uninsured have little option other than via the clinic emergency room or the city or county hospital. This is catch as catch can. The quality of care can vary from superlative to dismal. People caught in this awful situation usually do not know their rights. Another level is the health maintenance organization (HMO). Organizations like Kaiser Permanente offer full medical cover within a closed system. Generally, the services are covered; the choice of specific health provider is not. Even here, most members of HMO's are not aware of all their rights.

Finally, there is fee for service. Insurance coverage allows access to almost any provider, usually with a limited co-pay (a small amount you personally are responsible for). While providing the ability to research and utilize the top names in medical care, here too the limitations and rights are not fully comprehended by patients so lucky to have such freedom of choice.

Summary
1. The onset of a severe medical condition creates immediate problems – all of them the property of the affected individual.
2. Who to call or where to go can be the first panicky question?
3. Once into a system providing healthcare, ignorance of options and personal rights is often not recognized or considered.
4. Virtually every health system today is obsessed with cost containment. Denial of care is frequent. Even if better treatment options exist, you might be denied access.
5. There is a need to know and a need for help.
6. Before you are halfway done, the health systems are potentially converting their fiscal problems on to the nature and quality of care you receive.

The Tactics
Be like a boy scout – be prepared. Plan ahead for a future event that is as likely to happen as day follows night and night follows day.

1. Recognize that at any time you or a loved one could be hit with a major medical problem.
2. Check that your health insurance is intact and that you are aware and understand the details of your coverage.

3. If you have no insurance, check out options available to you in your city or community.

4. Recognize that when the problem hits, it is yours.

5. Ensure your health insurer does not burden you with their problem – advice easily given, certainly not simple to follow. But the best you can do is read the fine print in your health policy <u>before</u> illness occurs. Know your rights, obligations, portals of access, lines of communication and mechanisms for lodging complaints.

6. Get a family gatekeeper. This refers to a good General Practitioner (GP), Family Practitioner (FP), internist or OB/GYN providing primary care (all called PCP's – primary care physicians).

7. I would like to expand on the value of healthy living and preventive healthcare – perhaps I should leave that for another book at another time. But at least get regular check-ups, get to know your PCP and let your PCP get to know you!

8. If your problem develops slowly – learn about it – get material from your PCP, or use reliable web resources, the public library, consumer medical organizations and support groups. (Of course don't trust everything on the web, keep to legitimate sites).

9. When the bills come in, question all denials. Impersonal notices you get from the medical insurance are often routine – they are trying you for size. Lodge complaints in writing – get letters of support from your physician. With hospital related issues, get the hospital accounting

department on your side. There is a lot of help there – just don't let the medical insurance company deny you any of your rights under your contract. Remember, they are attempting to convert their fiscal problem into your problem.

3. Being the Caregiver to Someone Else with Severe Disease or Disability

I prefer to address this issue with a case illustration.

I discovered examples of such problems in my medical practice every time I was in the office. Take the case of Maria X.

Maria is single, 61, living with her mother age 82. Her office appointments for her regular check-ups are spent more in discussions about her domestic circumstances than her health. And that in itself is a problem!

She has a very demanding mother who expects her to be home as daughter, nurse, caretaker, cook, general bottle washer and everything else. "You have put on too much weight and your unhealthy cholesterol is higher than it should be " I tell her, and she responds, "I know, I am so busy with mother and my job, I have no time for myself." So she gets herself fatter, sicker, sadder and lonelier. Hers is a frequent story in my office. "You know, I advise her, you really need to care for yourself first. What good is a sick caretaker?" She nods in agreement, but I know that this simple piece of advice, though believed, will be ignored. So what can I do better to help her resolve this situation?

I explain to her the issue of "problem ownership." We go through a long conversation – "your mother's demands and needs are her problem – and she has successfully made her problem your problem." "Yes, mother has money to hire a part-time nurse; yes, my two brothers and sister are also in Cleveland and leave everything to me and don't spend much time with mother." "Yes, I would like to take classes at the local university; yes, I would like to exercise; yes, I would like to spend time on myself; yes, I am lonely and would like to date, but mother. . ."

We discuss problem identification. I counsel her on putting her foot down with mother and siblings; tell them that "mother has made her problem completely mine, but it isn't. If we are to assume ownership of the problem, then ownership is going to be shared. Yes, all of us are going to split obligations. I am taking some time out for myself – what I plan to do is my business not your business." I asked her to promise me she will have this conversation.

Six months later I see Maria. She has met a man, also attending evening classes at the university. "Do you think I could still have intercourse at my age"? "What about Mother? Oh yes, that advice worked, we are all spending time with her, and the part-time housekeeper is doing much of the necessary."

Maria has lost weight, has had her hair done, is using cosmetics – looks and behaves like a different woman. Life for her has begun at 60. She gave up ownership on someone else's problem, worked her way through the situation, and has transformed her future.

Take-Away Messages

1. A personal health problem is unfortunately primarily a personal problem.
2. That being accepted, it can then be a problem shared.

3. But both sides need to recognize that aspects of the problem differ depending upon which side of the fence you sit.

4. Make yourself aware of all treatment options, and utilize all the resources available to you

5. Be aware of the status of your health insurance, especially understanding what the insurance covers.

6. Don't hesitate to query invoices, and to utilize the assistance of your doctor's office or hospital accounts department.

7. Do not allow the insurance company to convert their fiscal problems into your problem.

Chapter 6

The Inverse Utian Strategy – Your Pathway to Success

Call it hypocrisy, but turning The Utian Strategy on its head could be an effective mechanism to success. Simply, persuade someone else that your problem is actually his or her problem! This is where the salesman in you has to come into play. Certainly it is selfish. But it can be a good means to a positive end.

The Strategy

1. Identify your problem.
2. Consider how to convince the opposite party that your problem is really their problem, even though its resolution would personally benefit you.
3. Go for it.

Illustrations

1. Enhance your travel experience

I travel widely, have done so for many years, and have become particularly comfortable in analyzing and communicating with hotel front desk assistants and floor managers. We are all aware of the fact that hotels have rooms of different grades, sizes, better views, bigger bathrooms, or quieter positions. When I check in, I greet the front desk assistant warmly, say how pleased I am at last to be in the hotel and ask if I am getting the best available non-smoking king-bed room. On the way to the room I engage the bellman in friendly conversation and make a point of asking if the hotel is full. When I get to the room he asks the usual question like "does the room satisfy you?" My immediate response is always "are there better rooms?"

If dissatisfied with the room, I activate the Inverse Utian Strategy – make my problem of dissatisfaction with the room, the front desk assistant or hotel manager's problem.

The conversation, after I have politely introduced myself, usually goes something like this "you have a wonderful property, but unfortunately the room I have just been allocated does not reflect that. You know, I travel frequently, and use this hotel chain a lot. Certainly, you would not want to leave me with a bad impression."

The Tactics

1. I recognize the problem.
2. I lay a guilt trip on the shoulders of the hotel official, leading them to believe they have created the problem – allocating me an unsatisfactory room.
3. Then I smile disarmingly, say little more, and wait.
4. If the hotel is not full – it works every time.

Commentary

This is a really an extremely simple example in which the problem bounces, gets resolved, no one loses, and certainly I gain.

Children inherently learn this technique at a very early age. They want something, have it denied by one parent, catch the other parent off guard, and leave both parents with their problem, while they move on to other mischief. Parents have to wise up early, be on the same page; otherwise they will become even more frequent victims of problem transference.

2. *Offer your problem as a benefit to the presenter*

Example 1: Be Tom Sawyer
There are in fact situations where you can pass your problem on in a way that makes the presenter of the problem really believe that assuming ownership is to their benefit. Mark Twain gave the best example of all time to us years ago. Remember when Tom Sawyer is presented with a problem by his aunt to whitewash the fence. Tom was interested in resting in the shade and the last thing on his mind was to paint a fence in the hot sunshine. What did he do? He pretended that his assignment was something of great value, and in the end he had his friends lining up to grab the paint brush, indeed pay him with their valuable objects for the privilege, while he observed in comfort from the shade.

Now of course there really was no value to Tom's friends in picking up his dirty work, so we can say that this was a devious way around despite its success. But there are other ways that really can be win-win for both parties.

Here is another personal story. I was faced with a problem way back in the early days of my OB/GYN residency when I first moved to Cape Town. One of my first assignments was to be the co-resident with an extremely lazy individual at a hospital in District 6, a part of Cape Town that was rough, densely populated, vibrant, colorful, dangerous, exciting, and challenging. At the time the apartheid Nationalist government in South Africa was legislating the razing of the District and removal of the population to a desolate wind-swept area miles out of the City. They eventually achieved this, and even to this day, weeds grow over an area that was historic and had a unique architecture – a sad loss for all time. But that is not the story.

Peninsula Hospital was in the middle of District 6, and being a hospital designated for 'non-whites' was overloaded with patients and poorly supported financially by the government. This meant that we medical residents worked extremely hard under difficult circumstances. Indeed, we worked 36 hours on call and 12 hours off, and the process was relentless.

Imagine what it was like then with your co-resident trying to shirk every duty going. One thankless task was to be responsible for producing the on-call roster for all the interns and medical students. As with most things, I was handed the responsibility. I did a 'Tom Sawyer" on my colleague. When he smirked at me after I was handed the assignment, I looked at him, smiled, and said that I had been given an amazing opportunity of working the roster to my advantage. He blinked, and amazingly, offered to take over the responsibility. I relinquished 'reluctantly', although of course with our work roster of on 36 hours/ off 12 meant there was really nothing he could do to change things for either of us.

Example 2: Truly offer a problem as a benefit
There are times at home or at work where a problem that is truly yours can be given to the opposite party and where they could in fact benefit.

Home: A patient of mine related an experience to me that fits under this category. She was a stay at home Mom and desperately wanted time out and away from the children. Her husband was hardworking, and an avid golfer. She wanted to go to an art class on a Wednesday afternoon, the mid-week afternoon he played golf. She realized this was her problem, although I think it could be debated. Nonetheless, instead of confronting him in a hostile way, she played on his emotions and laid a guilt trip on him. She related how quickly the children were growing, how her poor husband was missing out on the milestones and things the children were doing after school, and how one afternoon a week would make such a difference to his life and theirs. He bought the sob story, gave up Wednesday golf, and spends the afternoon with his kids. Her final comment to me was that her husband had told her that Wednesday afternoons had become the most enjoyable part of the week. Win-win!

Lesson: Think your problems through. Don't challenge or confront the opposite party. Rather work out how you can sell the problem as a benefit.

Work: At one time of my career I was running the equivalent of 5 full time jobs (academic department Chair, hospital department Director, clinical practice manager, practicing reproductive endocrinologist, and Executive Director of a non-profit medical society). If I had to resolve all the problems I was faced with I could never have got a day done. So I learned the diplomatic (or political?) language of explaining to individuals, once we had agreed a problem they had brought to me was mine, that despite the fact of ownership, their assumption of the problem could be a learning experience, offer a personal benefit, or even be a career enhancer. There are multiple examples to illustrate this approach. Take one like the junior faculty person who had brought to my attention that there was a problem with the teaching program for the medical students. At the time, Department Directors at the medical school were the point persons for setting up the program. I explained to my faculty member that her assuming the responsibility for program development, and coming to me towards the end of the process to offer comment, review or refine, would really ultimately be to her benefit. It turned out that way, and a large component of her future career became focused on education.

Conclusion

There are valid circumstances in which it is okay for you to try and make your problem belong to the opposite party, and the outcome can very often benefit both sides.

Chapter 7

Tell Them It Is Their Problem – Fix It!

And then came Covid 19. Maybe China mishandled the onset and misled the world. Maybe the United States should have realized earlier that the virus was entering the country with Western European tourists. Maybe… All irrelevant and off the point in regard to our own lives as we currently live them.

The fact is that these arguments and questions are entirely unrelated to what we are all dealing with right now, indeed any major regional or national problem. They can be argued and discussed by commissions of enquiry for years to come, letting the world learn how mistakes were made all round, and how they can be avoided in the future. For now we have to deal with a specific situation, each in our own way. But we are entitled to ask questions and seek remedies. The owner of the problem has to be identified, and that owner needs to come up with scientifically designed and practical remedies.

So, we have a Covid-19 pandemic and are all concerned about being infected. And we have an economic depression, and each in our own way has to work out how to survive and move forward.

The problem: An epidemic caused by the Covid-19 virus that has spread worldwide and that affects different individuals in extremes ranging from being asymptomatic to dying, with gradations of severity of symptoms in-between, not to mention the socio-economic impact, the effect on children and their education, psycho-social trauma and the rest.

Whose problem is it? In a perverse way, it is all of our problem. That is not to say we all own all of the problem. Indeed, there is in fact not a single 'Covid problem.'

What then are the 'Covid problems?

The disease itself: No one wants to catch it, but if we do, the problem of treating and healing us rests on the shoulders of our brave health-care workers. They weren't asking for it, but by the very fact they chose to be healthcare providers, means they accept responsibility for treating the illness as best as possible. This part of the problem they own.

Avoiding the disease: Here I believe we own the problem. How assiduously we obey the best scientific advice of hand hygiene, social distancing, wearing masks, avoiding crowds especially indoors, cleaning surfaces, and so on, and eventually getting vaccinated against Covid, are all our personal responsibility. If we break the rules we actually deserve the consequences.

Preventing the disease: Disease prevention is part of good governance. We elect our local, regional and national officials with a rather narrow set of mandates. Above all they take an oath to protect and defend us. That means that the problem of identifying risks of new diseases, mechanisms for mitigating their spread, obtaining and/or creating preventives against the new invader like vaccines, and treatments for when the disease impacts, are all problems that belong fair and square on the shoulders of those officials. The dismal failure of the response in the United States starts at the top down. By contrast, a country like South Africa starting with massive areas of abject poverty, because of good governance, at least in this instance, was able to control the pandemic and flatten the curve.

Treating the disease: As mentioned, this is the problem for the healthcare industry. Hopefully, one way or another, we are financially insured against the costs, but that is another problem.

The problem of problem owners not taking ownership of their problem

Our officials: Under lockdown the one commodity we all found to have more than we would have liked was time. I am sure many of you were like me, and watched the TV news to excess. One thing that became abundantly clear was that far too many of our elected officials were ducking and weaving every which way not to take any ownership of the problem. I don't need to expand. You know what I mean. The lies, the obfuscations, the conspiracy theories, the snake oil remedies they touted, the avoidance of science-based guidelines, the blame-game, the list goes on and on.

The remedy for bad public servants: Simple. The ballot boxes. Kick the bums out.

Individual deniers and conspiracy theorists: Sometime during the first few weeks of lockdown I went to my local supermarket to stock up on supplies. I was pleasantly surprised to find out how well prepared they were – my temperature taken at the door, hands sprayed with sanitizer, and limited customers at a time. At the cashier line there were 2-meter spaced marks on the floor to indicate the need for social distancing. To my annoyance, the woman in line behind me was literally breathing down my neck. Each time I moved forward she did the same. Eventually I turned around and said, "Please madam, the markers on the floor mean we need to socially distance." Her angry rejoinder was, "Oh, that's been government gazetted has it!" I responded, "No, it is for your safety and for my safety." She turned red in the face and stepped back. The point is that bad behavior happens. She was making her problem mine, and my reaction was to hand the problem right back to her.

Conclusion

Sometimes, perhaps once in a lifetime, a problem hits everyone simultaneously and appears to have no ownership or solution. Covid-19 is such a problem. But even a complex problem like the Covid-19 pandemic needs to be carefully considered and broken down into its essentials. How many problems does it create, whose problems are they, how do we ensure that ownership of the specific problem is appropriately assumed, and how do we avoid transference of other 's share of the problem being thrust on us or threatening us with a negative impact? Even here, the Utian Strategy works.

Chapter 8

Summing Up the Utian Strategy

So there you have it. In a nutshell, I have shared my most personal technique for success.

The **principles** of the Utian Strategy are always the same.

The approach you take, the **tactics**, can, and almost always, differ.

The Utian Strategy - Principles

1. Be aware of problems all around you, but especially the one that is coming right at you. Recognize the existence of a problem immediately. Alternatively, recognize that a situation, the problem, is possibly impending or developing.
2. Dissect the problem to its core elements – what exactly is the problem?
3. Ask the key questions – "is this my problem or is this your problem?" Whose problem is this?
4. Identify the owner – you or the opposite party.
5. Ascribe ownership – make it clear you are accepting the problem, or inform the opposite party that it is their problem to deal with and resolve.

6. If the problem is yours, resolve your problem.

7. If the problem belongs to the opposite party by all means be prepared to offer advice to the problem owner within limits – just don't accept ownership if the problem is not yours.

8. If the other party will not accept responsibility, shrug your shoulders, tell them that it is really their problem and walk away.

9. Always expect the least from those that you have helped the most – that way you will not be disillusioned or disappointed.

The Utian Strategy - Tactics

To achieve success with the Utian Strategy, you must understand that tactics can differ. The following are some of the lessons I have learned along the way and have mentioned before in the various case studies:

1. It is very simple to advise someone else what to do; following your own advice is not that easy.

2. The Utian Strategy will not work if you allow yourself to get emotionally involved. Keep your cool! The closer you are to the other party, the more difficult this is.

3. Trying too hard to assist the problem owner in resolving their problem can result in their problem becoming your problem. Control your involvement – stay aware of the prime issue.

4. When emotion creeps in, try and call a time out - an opportunity for re-gathering thoughts and getting back on track.

5. Bite your tongue - errors of commission are worse than errors of omission. Words said in anger cannot be taken back.

6. Learn when to listen. Someone may just want a sounding board to bounce the problem off and may not really be looking for a new owner.

7. Some problems should be co-owned.

8. Compromise can be acceptable, particularly in family issues, when sharing the burden can ease the load.

9. An observer – especially one in an influential position - can recognize a problem between two parties and play an important role as a referee.

10. The reluctant owner of a problem might need to have a resolution forced on him or her.

11. Sometimes you have no alternate to accepting ownership of someone else's problem. But when you do, go in with eyes wide open. Know what you are accepting.

12. Recognize the elements of the problem and in planning a solution, work towards the best possible outcome of those elements.

13. Results may not always be perfect, but they should at least be acceptable.

14. Be alert for all innuendos and signals in verbal and body language.

15. Be certain that people you think are on your side are actually and really on your side.

16. Accepting promotion, directorship of a department or company, or, indeed any new position of responsibility, brings with it ownership of existing problems. That is why you are being appointed. You had better identify existing problems before signing the dotted line – after that they are all yours!

17. Stick to your principles.

18. Transference of ownership can sometimes be achieved without any discussion.

19. A team approach to resolving problems can simplify the process.

20. One problem can sometimes be replaced by another. Stay alert for the change.

21. The problem can swing from party to party like a tennis ball. Keep your eye on the ball.

22. Watch out for subplots.

23. Educate staff and colleagues to recognize that problem ownership is key to problem resolution.

24. You can profit by persuading someone else that your problem is his or hers. There are valid circumstances for this transference.

25. In tense, complex family conflicts problem ownership belongs to all. When emotion trumps cool discussion, the Utian Strategy does not work. At least seek the services of a family counselor.

In Conclusion

Always work out: *Is this my problem or is this your problem?*

Always tell the other party: *Don't make your problem my problem!*

Always keep your eye on the prize: *Just get the problem resolved, move on with life, and take time out to smell the roses!*

Try and reverse the situation and get rid of the problem! Then it is their problem and not yours. Of course, they may also have read this book, and that should make for an interesting competition!

Life is what is happening while you are making other plans

– John Lennon.

Notes

How to Order

To order this book go to most online booksellers including www.amazon.com and enter the author's name, Wulf Utian, in the search box. Click on the book's title when the page comes up to access details and ordering information.

To order bulk print copies email: wulf@utianllc.com

If you found *THE UTIAN STRATEGY* to be of value, please post a review for it on Amazon.com.

Share An Experience of Your Own

We all have unique experiences that have lessons to teach or to learn. **If you have an interesting story to share, please email me at:** wulf@utianllc.com

You can also **blog a comment** through my website on one of the subjects under the heading WHAT'S UP at: www.UtianLLC.com

www.ingramcontent.com/pod-product-compliance
Lightning Source LLC
Chambersburg PA
CBHW070738020526
44118CB00035B/1601